Asteroids Our Cosmic Influencers

B D SALERNO

Published by B D SALERNO, 2024.

While every precaution has been taken in the preparation of this book, the publisher assumes no responsibility for errors or omissions, or for damages resulting from the use of the information contained herein.

ASTEROIDS OUR COSMIC INFLUENCERS

First edition. December 30, 2024.

Copyright © 2024 B D SALERNO.

ISBN: 979-8988478560

Written by B D SALERNO.

Also by B D SALERNO

Desperate Rites
Desperate Rites: Astrology and the Occult in the Richard Speck Murders

Standalone
Richard Speck and the Eight Nurses: Deconstructing A Mass Murder
Richard Speck and the Eight Nurses: Deconstructing A Mass Murder
Anywhere But Here: Confessions of A Pisces Moon
Asteroids Our Cosmic Influencers

ACKNOWLEDGMENT

I extend my sincere thanks to my sister and fellow astrologer, Cheryl Salerno, former editor of the Association for Research and Enlightenment Press, whose helpful suggestions, keen sense of humor, and very sharp proofreader's pencil helped bring this idea to fruition.

B D SALERNO

FOREWORD

Before the year 1990, an astrology ephemeris might not contain asteroids, except for perhaps Chiron (also spelled Kiron). Since then, however, most ephemerides now include Chiron, Ceres, Pallas, Vesta, and Juno, as more astrologers are noting their influence in analyzing clients' charts.

But this is only the beginning. With over 1.2 million known asteroids and over 500,000 named asteroids now identified and tracked by various institutes and observatories, how can astrologers possibly begin to research – let alone understand – the dizzying array of energies streaking through space, sprinking their influence among the newborns on Earth?

The good news is that this reference book has identified over 400 of the oldest, best known, and most often referenced asteroids, giving a brief history and description of their influence. Also included are many examples of how our cosmic influencers have shown up in the natal charts of some really good – and really bad – people we know and love.

This might be only the first of such reference books, so stay tuned. There's so much more to know and be amazed by.

Cheryl Salerno December 30, 2024

ASTEROIDS OUR COSMIC INFLUENCERS

INTRODUCTION

As much as I love the study of astrology, there was always one subject that I avoided like the plague. That was the study of the asteroids. Those craggy chunks of rock and minerals, with their multiple mythological characters, symbols, and interpretations, literally put the fear of Zeus into me.

We already had CERES 1, PALLAS 2, JUNO 3, VESTA 4, and CHIRON 2060 when I was taking my first baby steps as an astrologer. In addition to learning the major planets, aspects, solar returns, progressions, profections, and the like, my mental bandwidth was already stretched to its snapping point. So for many years those mythical marauders remained as distant from my conscious mind as from planet Earth itself. And that was just fine with me!

But, as always happens with myths and melodramas, something else was working behind the scenes to finally force an astral reckoning: forensic astrology. The Regulus software that I use includes many asteroids, and once in a while I would check them against crime charts just out of curiosity (or some other persistent inner prompting).

Curiosity turned quickly to obsession when I saw how the asteroids filled in gaps of detail, lending color and backstory to an event like the dial on a receiver that allows you to pinpoint and then fine-tune the frequency.

Those intimidating chunks of rock that I had so studiously avoided suddenly came to life, and became indispensable to my practice. But then something else was missing: a concrete physical reference where I could get all the information about them in one place.

In researching the asteroids I often found it necessary to consult multiple online resources. Several astrology forums and websites, credited in the References section, were extremely informative and helpful to this end. But I saw the need for a physical desk reference – I must confess a love and preference for books over cyberspace - and that idea gave birth to this book.

There are just over 400 asteroids discussed here. As there are now over 500,000 named asteroids, I believe more volumes of this book will be forthcoming. In the meantime, I hope this directory will be helpful!

B.D. Salerno

December 30, 2024

ASTEROIDS OUR COSMIC INFLUENCERS

WHAT IS AN ASTEROID?

Think of an asteroid as a minor planet. That's what they used to be called until astronomy discovered just how many types and categories of minor planets there were in our solar system. Even as of this writing, more are being discovered, categorized, and defined.

Asteroids are basically chunks of rocks, minerals, or icy objects in space that orbit around the Sun as do the major planets. They vary greatly in size, composition, weight, and shape; some measure barely over a kilometer in width, while some, like Ceres, are among the largest.

What differentiates the asteroids from the planets is size. While Ceres remains one of the largest, she still measures only 1/13 of the size of Earth, so could not be considered a major planet, having a diameter of only 940 kilometers.

Most asteroids orbit the Sun from belts contained within the orbits of Mars and Jupiter; these are the Main Belt asteroids, and they occupy most of the entries in this book. As technology progressed, many more astral bodies came to be discovered in locations farther and farther away, going past the orbit of Neptune – Centaurs, Trans-Neptunian Objects, and Dwarf Planets. These are still generally considered asteroids by astrologers, but to avoid confusion when consulting other software and resources, I have defined the different groups below.

If you're not that interested in the categories and types of asteroids you can just skip the following sections.

Differentiate between asteroid types – location matters!

This is not a scientific treatment of the asteroids, but a quick and dirty science lesson here is beneficial. It is helpful to know the different classifications of minor planets because they are defined in specific groups; i.e., CYLLARUS 52975 is a centaur, not an asteroid, and will be listed as such.

I have broken them down into three very generalized groups: Main Belt Asteroids, Centaurs, and Trans-Neptunian Objects. These groups break down further into more specific groups but for our purposes I will briefly discuss just these three.

Main Belt Asteroids

These asteroids were the first to be discovered, as they are closest to Earth and were more easily visible to the early telescopic lens of the 19th Century. CERES 1, still the largest asteroid, was the first to be discovered by Italian priest and astronomer Giuseppe Piazzi in 1801, with Pallas, Vesta, and Juno following.

The Main Belt asteroids are all located between the orbits of Mars and Jupiter and, like the rest of the planets, they orbit the Sun. They complete their orbits within a few years, like the inner planets, and therefore resonate on a personal level, as do the inner, more personal planets Mercury, Venus, Mars, and Moon.

Since the vast majority of the asteroids in our system are Main Belters, I have not made that designation in the "Discovery" headline of each section; I have done that only to indicate the bodies described below.

Centaurs

The Centaurs are designated in the heading "Discovery" as "Centaur."

They orbit between Jupiter and Neptune, and therefore require a longer time to complete their orbit around the Sun. For example, CHIRON 2060 takes 50.65 years to complete its orbit. When in aspect with an outer planet, therefore, the effect is generational, as

ASTEROIDS OUR COSMIC INFLUENCERS

Chiron will aspect Uranus in a very large segment of the population at the same time.

In mythology the centaurs were half man and half beast, which gave them extraordinary strength, a deep connection to animals and the environment, raw primal desires, a warlike nature, and a keen sense of adventure. Some of the mythical centaurs were bad, and some, like Chiron, were very good. All had bigger-than-life qualities.

Trans-Neptunian Objects (TNO)

These are designated as "TNO" in the Discovery heading, and refer to bodies that orbit beyond Neptune in a belt of icy objects called the Kuiper Belt. Like Uranus, Neptune, and Pluto, these bodies may take centuries to orbit the Sun. And with their own eccentric orbits and trajectories, not answering gravitationally to anything else near them, some are real oddballs.

Dwarf planets, like Pluto, and semi-comets (damocloids) also make their home in Neptune's backyard. These have been designated as "Dwarf Planet" or "Damocloid." They are all part and parcel of an irregular band of jolly nonconformists that dance to their own astral tune. They are truly the outer "fringe" of our solar system!

These off-the-grid behaviors contribute in part to their interpretation, as I have noted eccentric qualities in individuals having prominent TNOs in their charts, especially in relation to their personal planets.

However, they also indicate that the individual is capable of connecting to consciousness beyond the normal, embracing and understanding highly spiritual concepts.

The designation "TNO/SDO" simply refers to Trans-Neptunian Object/Scattered Disk Object, which is another category of freakish and unpredictable behavior. A "cubewano," like BORASISI 66652, is another rebel body that orbits Neptune but is not controlled by its gravitational pull. I make a point of noting this because I believe behaviors and interpretation go hand in hand where these amazing – and amusing – bodies are concerned.

HOW TO WORK WITH ASTEROIDS

Here are a few helpful tips that will facilitate working with asteroids and searching for information on an asteroid if it isn't presented here.

How I do my charts

I use Regulus Platinum software, which has an asteroid menu along the lower left-hand side of the page on which the chart appears. If you click on the Asteroid section it will pull up a listing of about 100 asteroids along the right hand side of the page and their placement by degree and sign. You'll then have to match them to the planets in the chart, using a one degree orb.

When I want to really drill down and select the specific asteroids of my choice I use the marvelous software at www.serennu.com[1]. You can run your chart and its asteroid listings from the "Ephemeris" section whose link is atop the home page. It will not present a circular chart, just the placements by degree and sign. But first there are a few steps to note for this process.

To run the chart for asteroids you need the UT (Universal Time) for the birth or event time. You can find this by entering your chart data at www.astro.com[2].

On the Ephemeris page enter the date and UT – note carefully that you must list the DAY first, not the MONTH as we do here in the US! You can also add the location coordinates but this is not required.

---

1. http://www.serennu.com
2. http://www.astro.com

ASTEROIDS OUR COSMIC INFLUENCERS

What is required for extensive research, though, is a paid subscription, by month or year, and the $10 a month is really more than worth it.

The asteroid module will pull up at least a hundred asteroids, but you can fill in any asteroid you want by adding its number into a space that appears underneath the birth data. You can also check a box that allows you to pull up 1,000 asteroids! The pull-down menu allows you to list the asteroids by name, by degree/sign, by number, and several other options. This is good for when I only want to check one obscure asteroid that I know will not appear in the general list: I search it by 'Name' to find its degree/sign, then I toggle back to list the rest of the data by Zodiac/30 degrees so that I can immediately compare the results to that asteroid.

Further down the page there is a link that will bring you to alphabetical lists of thousands of asteroids from A to Z. This too is an invaluable tool when researching asteroids for a particular chart, or just to see what's out there. (Caution: The lists are truly staggering!)

Degree of aspect

I use a strict orb of one degree in measuring an aspect from planet to asteroid, Ascendant, Midheaven, or the Nodes.

Always include the asteroid number in your search.

Some software, like the wonderful search platform at www.serennu.com[3], requires the asteroid number when conducting a search. It's also helpful if you are searching for astronomical information in www.wikipedia.org or www.minorplanetcenter.org[4] where literally hundreds of thousands of asteroids are listed in blocks

---

3. http://www.serennu.com

4. http://www.minorplanetcenter.org

of numbers, not names. Always make it a habit to include the number with the name if you plan on doing research.

Research the history, mythology, and any other related information in order to arrive at a meaning for an asteroid.

Somewhat magically, the earlier asteroids named for mythical gods and goddesses have the uncanny ability to describe persons in ways similar to the soap opera myth after which they were named. For example, many rock stars who have the asteroid ORPHEUS 3361 prominent in their charts led tumultuous lives followed by untimely, tragic deaths, as noted in this work.

Also, as I have so often pointed out in the book, some asteroids are as literal as they sound, like LIE 26955 and SWINDLE 8690, which were initially named for scientists bearing those surnames. Same applies to ANGA 3158 and PECKER 1629, among others.

Interpreting the asteroids

The first several hundred asteroids, discovered in the 19th Century, were named after characters from Greek and Roman mythology, and all of them were female. Thus, there are goddesses, monsters, evil queens, sorceresses and the like in the mix. Studying the mythical stories behind these characters is key to understanding what the asteroids are trying to tell us about the situations in the client's natal chart.

Many early astronomers also sought to honor their wives, mothers, and sisters (and the occasional mother-in-law) by naming asteroids after them. Often a person bearing a name similar or identical to an asteroid name will have that asteroid prominent in their chart! Not always, but it's fun to check. People may have names of other important individuals in their charts as well.

ASTEROIDS OUR COSMIC INFLUENCERS

The same applies to locations. The early astronomers, when not trying to impress or pacify their relatives or significant others by naming asteroids after them, also named asteroids after cities, provinces, and countries, like GERMANIA 241 or AUSONIA 63. These locationally named asteroids will often turn up in charts of people who have a vested interest in that city or country – in traveling there, living there, or studying the history, culture, or language of that location.

This is also important in event and forensic horoscopes where a city or location may give a crucial clue; i.e., if the perpetrator was a foreigner, or used a particular name. It's always interesting to test out the names and locations and see what turns up.

For example, I was intrigued by asteroid ARETHUSA 95 (not included in this text). It aspected a personal planet in the chart of R&B legend Aretha Franklin, but the orb was two degrees, so I didn't include the asteroid in this writing. However, it was still exciting to find Arethusa (Areth-USA) well-placed in the chart of an American R&B legend named Aretha! These celestial bodies can be as amusing as they are enlightening and informative.

And now for the asteroids ....

B D SALERNO

ABKHAZIA 2671

Discovery: August 21, 1977 by Nikolai Chernykh.

Backstory: Named after a region of the country of Georgia in Eastern Europe between the Black Sea and the Caucasus Mountains. The Abkhaz were an ancient indigenous people that inhabited the eastern shore of the Black Sea.

Possible Interpretation: While this asteroid is very specific in its reference, it may indicate an ancestral connection to that part of Europe or an interest in the culture, history, or language of the region; one's tribal roots.

Since the history of the region and its people has long been under dispute, the asteroid may also suggest enmity between ancestral or family members.

Example: In the natal chart of Russian President Vladimir Putin, Venus at 11 Scorpio opposes Abkhazia at 10 Taurus.

ABUNDANTIA 151

Discovery: November 1, 1875 by Johann Palisa.

Backstory: Minor Roman goddess of fertility and plenty; in Latin means "abundance."

Possible Interpretation: Shows where we are bountiful, where we accumulate wealth in its various forms (or don't).

Examples: In the natal chart of psychic medium Edgar Cayce, Abundantia exactly conjoins the South Node in 10 Virgo. He lived modestly, never charging money for his readings, and emphasized that abundance comes in many forms other than financial wealth.

ASTEROIDS OUR COSMIC INFLUENCERS

In the natal chart of Amazon.com billionaire Jeff Bezos, Venus at 24 Aquarius trines Abundantia at 23 Gemini.

ACHAEMENIDES 5126

Discovery: February 1, 1989 by Carolyn Shoemaker.

Backstory: He was a shipmate of Aeneas during his sea voyage to Carthage. He was left on the island with the terrifying Cyclops monster while everyone else from his ship managed to escape. Finally he was rescued by Aeneas.

Possible Interpretation: May represent where one is saved from a difficult situation, where someone benefits from the kindness of others.

Example: In the natal chart of celebrity Sean Combs, a.k.a "P. Diddy," Venus at 22 Libra sextiles Achaemenides at 22 Sagittarius. Some years ago he dodged a murder charge through the support of friends.

ACHILLES 588

Discovery: Discovered on February 22, 1906 by Max Wolf.

Backstory: Achilles was a Greek heroic leader who devised the idea of hiding Greek warriors inside a hollow wooden horse, which was then offered to, and accepted by, the leaders of Troy, only to be slain in the middle of the night when the warriors exited the horse and wreaked havoc upon the city. Troy was subsequently defeated when Achilles slew Hector, one of their main leaders.

Possible Interpretation: Shows where the person is physically or emotionally vulnerable, as was the heel of Achilles, and signals areas of weakness in the physical or emotional constitution.

Examples: In the natal chart of former Italian Prime Minister Aldo Moro, who was kidnapped and murdered by terrorists in 1978, Mars at 9 Scorpio trines Achilles at 10 Cancer; the kidnappers found a weak spot in his security detail.

Disgraced former governor Mario Cuomo of New York, who was forced to resign due to fallout from the COVID scandal, has his 16 Sagittarius Saturn exactly conjunct Achilles.

Stunt daredevil Evil Knievel has his 13 Leo Moon in exact trine with Achilles in Aries. Although his feats thrilled the public for many years, he suffered numerous injuries, breaking nearly every bone in his body during his career.

Influential Washington, D.C. attorney Ken Starr, who led the failed impeachment attempt of then-President Bill Clinton, has Achilles exactly conjunct his South Node at 20 Sagittarius.

ADEONA 145

Discovery: Discovered June 3, 1875 by Christian Peters.

Backstory: Roman goddess of homecomings.

Possible Interpretation: Shows where we connect to nostalgia, a sense of home, where we feel most comfortable; a connection to ancestry.

ADMETE 398

Discovery: December 28, 1894 by Auguste Charlois. There is also a Uranian planet, Admetos, which appears without a number.

Backstory: Admete was a King of Pherae in Thessaly who, upon learning that he had only a short time to live, sought the counsel of his friend Apollo to try and cheat death. Apollo asked the Moirai to grant Admete a longer life, but of course, a deal had to be made: Admete could be spared provided someone else gave their life in his place. This loving sacrifice was made by his wife, Alcestis, who died in order to spare her husband. She was later brought back from death by Heracles.

There is confusion among the names Admete, Admetis, and Admetos, furthered by the existence of a Trans-Neptunian Object (TNO) named Admetos 85030. I believe they all refer to the Thessalian king Admetus, so the interpretations would stay the same. If the reader finds differently, I would welcome the correction at the contact information provided in the notes to this book.

Possible Interpretation: The story lends itself to the interpretation of a person for whom others are willing to work hard, sacrifice their time, affections, efforts, and even lives. A person of influence who receives valuable assistance from their associates in times of need.

Example: Dr. Jack Kevorkian, called the "doctor of death" because he participated in assisted suicides of terminally ill patients, had Venus at 25 Taurus (Algol) in direct opposition to Admete.

In the natal chart of actress Nicole Kidman, North Node at 5 Taurus sextiles Admete at 5 Cancer.

ADONIS 2101

Discovery: February 12, 1936 by Eugène Joseph Delporte.

Backstory: Adonis was the embodiment of the perfect young male in beauty and physique; he is the son of Myrrha who also appears in these pages. See MYRRHA 381. Because he was so handsome, both Aphrodite and Persephone were besotted with him, but sadly, he was killed by a boar while hunting. So distraught was Aphrodite that she complained to the Fates, who then allowed that the anemone flower might grow from his blood.

Possible Interpretation: Adonis may indicate a very attractive, sensual person, someone who is sought after and desired by others; he also represents resurrection, as his blood gave birth to flowers.

Example: John F. Kennedy Jr., late son of the late President JFK, had Uranus at 25 Leo square Adonis at 24 Scorpio.

ADRASTEA 239

Discovery: August 18, 1884 by Johann Palisa.

Backstory: A mountain deity from the area of northwestern Turkey who represents the concept of Necessity and defends the righteous.

Possible Interpretation: Shows where we get stuck in situations that are difficult to leave, where we struggle to overcome problems due to past trauma or abuse; where we strive to do the right thing or to support those who are righteous.

Example: Popular singer Taylor Swift has Venus at 1 Aquarius in exact square to Adrastea at 1 Scorpio.

In the natal chart of Indian spiritual leader and activist Mahatma Gandhi, Adrastea exactly opposes his 25 Libra Ascendant.

AESCULAPIA 1027

Discovery: November 11, 1923 by George van Biesbroeck.

Backstory: Aesculapius was the god of medicine in Greek mythology.

Possible Interpretation: The asteroid signifies resurrection, healing from injury or trauma, or where one makes major transformative changes.

Examples: This asteroid is prominent in the chart of Twentieth Century psychic and trance medium Edgar Cayce (1877-1945), who delivered nearly 10,000 health and medical readings to people all over the world, many of which were documented as successful in restoring the individual to good health.

Less helpful, unfortunately, is the placement of Aesculapia in the natal chart of Dr. Anthony Fauci, where the asteroid conjoins the malefic fixed star Caput Algol at 26 Taurus. Fauci's Aesculapia also forms a trine to Neptune at 27 Virgo.

AGLAEA 47 [AGLAJA]

Discovery: September 15, 1857 by Robert Luther.

Backstory: Along with Thalia and Euphrosyne she is one of the Three Charities and is usually depicted holding a mirror that reflects the light of the sun, moon, stars, and flowers. She is associated with beauty and one's outward projection of self.

Possible Interpretation: Shows where one may become more beautiful, more beloved, more popular, or actually engage in these areas for business purposes, such as owning a beauty salon.

Example: Actress Jennifer Aniston has Jupiter at 5 Libra square Aglaea at 6 Capricorn.

AGNI 398188

Discovery: June 3, 2010 by WISE [Wide-field Infrared Survey Explorer].

Backstory: Agni is a Pancha Bhuta god and son of Brahma. He is said to have sprung from the mouth of the Cosmic Man after being born from Brahma.

Possible Interpretation: May represent our desire to commit and connect to Source; our drive for self-development and enlightenment.

B D SALERNO

AKHENATEN 326290

Discovery: April 21, 1988 by R. Tucker.

Backstory: An Egyptian pharaoh who led the cult of worship of the sun god Aten.

Possible Interpretation: Greatness and success; devotion to a higher being.

ALBION 15760

Discovery: August 30, 1992 by David C. Jewitt and Jane X. Luu. TNO.

Backstory: The first trans-Neptunian object to be discovered after Pluto/Charon, Albion was first nicknamed "Smiley" but that was withdrawn in view of the earlier asteroid Smiley 1613. Albion is a derivation of the Latin word for white and was at one time a mythical name for Britain. It made its way into a poem by Romantic poet William Blake in which Albion was a giant who represented the human race.

Possible Interpretation: Indicates an attachment to strong beliefs, a desire to encompass and unify different groups or cultures, someone who stands for something bigger than themselves.

Examples: In the natal chart of JonBenet Ramsey, Jupiter at 27 Cancer exactly trines Albion at 27 Pisces. Her tragic murder unified the nation in grief and brought attention to the shady world of child beauty pageants.

In the natal chart of multi-billionaire Warren Buffett, Mercury at 3 Libra partile squares Albion in Capricorn.

ASTEROIDS OUR COSMIC INFLUENCERS

Popular sitcom actor Matthew Perry had Sun at 26 Leo partile opposite Albion.

Seven-time Super Bowl champion quarterback Tom Brady has Albion at 8 Pisces exactly opposite his Mercury.

ALETHEIA 259

Discovery: June 28, 1886 by Christian Peters.

Backstory: Greek goddess of truth, representing the "Pursuit of Truth, Identity and Remembrance."

Possible Interpretation: As it sounds – someone desirous of seeking or exposing the truth; justice, fairness and balance in matters; possibly involved in some way with the law.

Example: Chief Justice of SCOTUS Samuel Alito has Jupiter at 27 Aquarius square Aletheia at 26 Taurus.

ALICANTO 474640

Discovery: November 6, 2004 by A.C. Becker. TNO.

Backstory: The alicanto is an nocturnal exotic bird in Chilean mythology whose multi-colored bright wings illuminate the skies in the Atacama desert.

Possible Interpretation: The alicanto represents a guiding light in the darkness, and so indicates where we may find enlightenment, healing, self-improvement, the pot of gold at the end of the rainbow.

Example: In the natal chart of Eugenie, Princess of York, Mercury at 7 Aries partile conjoins Alicanto.

ALKESTE 124 [also ALCESTIS]

B D SALERNO

Discovery: August 23, 1882 by Christian Peters.

Backstory: Greek wife of Admetos who offered herself up to die in his place. See also ADMETE 398.

Possible Interpretation: May reference a giving, sacrificial nature; where we give ourselves up for others; where we may be called upon to sacrifice for someone perhaps less deserving; a martyr complex.

Examples: In the event chart of the reported kidnapping of JonBenet Ramsey, the Sun at 5 Capricorn partile squares Alkeste in Aries.

In the natal chart of actress Ali MacGraw, her 19 Taurus Ascendant trines Alkeste at 19 Virgo. She divorced actor Steve McQueen after several years of an abusive, volatile marriage.

Indian spiritual leader and activist Mahatma Gandhi had the Sun at 8 Libra square Alkeste at 8 Cancer.

ALKMENE 82

Discovery: November 27, 1864 by Robert Luther.

Backstory: Mother of Herakles [Hercules] who was seduced by Zeus and then blamed and disgraced by her husband.

Possible Interpretations: May reference a similar scenario of a seduction, unfair accusations, or infidelity; where situations are out of one's control.

Example: In the natal chart of actor George Clooney, his 27 Capricorn Moon trines Alkmene at 28 Taurus.

ALONA 15230

Discovery: September 13, 1987 by Henri Debehonge.

ASTEROIDS OUR COSMIC INFLUENCERS

Backstory: Named after the daughter of Valentin Arkadievna Andreichenko, who performed measurements for the discoverer and also acted as translator.

Possible Interpretation: References where we stand on our own, where we seek solitude; also, a sense of alienation, loneliness. May not just be about loneliness, as it could also indicate where we stand alone in our accomplishments as leaders or examples.

ALTJIRA 148780

Discovery: October 20, 2001 by Marc Buie. TNO.

Backstory: It is a deity of the Arrernte aboriginal people of Australia who believe that Altjira created the earth during the Dreamtime and then departed to take up residence in the heavens. Altjira is a Kuiper Belt object.

Possible Interpretation: Unlike many of its asteroid colleagues it is found just outside the orbit of Neptune and so may relate to higher consciousness, a deep universal connection, or on the other hand, deception, illusion, and trickery. If well aspected may instead describe higher levels of spiritual development and an ability to accurately interpret dreams. Also, if well aspected, shows the manifestation of creativity through achieving one's dreams.

Examples: In the natal chart of Princess Diana, Mercury at 3 Cancer squares Altjira at 3 Aries.

Supermodel Gisele Bundchen has her Sun at 28 Cancer in square to Altjira at 28 Aries.

Walt Disney, famous producer of animated cartoons, had his 9 Libra Moon in square to Altjira at 9 Capricorn. His studio theme song was "When You Wish Upon a Star."

AMALTHEA 113

Discovery: March 12, 1871 by Robert Luther.

Backstory: Greek nursemaid who tended to baby Zeus.

Possible Interpretation: Caretakers, helpers, nurses, healers, those who provide service to others.

Examples: Chief Justice of SCOTUS Antonin Scalia had Mercury at 26 Aquarius square Amalthea at 26 Taurus.

Los Angeles celebrity defense attorney Mark Geragos, who defended Scott Peterson and Winona Ryder, has a 0 Libra Ascendant trine Amalthea at 0 Gemini.

AMAZONE 1042

Discovery: April 22, 1925 by Karl Wilhelm Reinmuth.

Backstory: Named in honor of the Amazon women of Greek lore, upon which the contemporary Wonder Woman series was based. See HIPPOLYTA 10295.

Possible Interpretation: May indicate a superior athlete; an imposing figure; a very independent nature that does not easily commit in relationships.

Example: Award-winning actress Allison Janney, who is six feet tall, has her Neptune at 7 Scorpio partile conjuct Amazone.

AMBROSIA 193

Discovery: February 28, 1879 by Jérome Cöggia.

Backstory: Greek food or "nectar" of the gods.

ASTEROIDS OUR COSMIC INFLUENCERS

Possible Interpretation: References where one experiences delight and sustenance, be it in food, drink, or material pleasures, or in deeper spiritual attunement.

AMICITIA 367

Discovery: May 19, 1893 by Auguste Charlois.

Backstory: Latin word for friendship.

Possible Interpretation: How and where the person establishes friendships easily, whether things go smoothly with friends (or not) and how much he values friendship (or doesn't).

Example: In the natal chart of actor/director/producer Clint Eastwood, Mars at 28 Aries sextiles Amicitia at 28 Aquarius.

AMOR 1221

Discovery: March 12, 1932 by Eugène Delporte.

Backstory: This asteroid is part of a belt of approximately 12,020 asteroids of the same name. Amor is the Roman god of love, adapted from the Greek Eros and depicted as a young man with wings. His love match is the goddess Psyche, whom he first awoke from sleep with a kiss.

Possible Interpretations: Amor shows the person's ideal of love, how they express kindness and affection, what and who attracts them; our vulnerabilities in love.

Examples: In the natal chart of serial pedophile Jeffrey Epstein, Amor at 16 Taurus is conjunct Nessus at 14 Taurus. He was enamored of seducing underage girls by offering them jobs and money, and is profiled below in a number of places, all of them unsavory. See NESSUS 7066.

B D SALERNO

In the natal chart of serial rapist/killer/cannibal Jeffrey Dahmer, Amor at 4 Taurus forms a grand trine with Jupiter at 2 Capricorn and Pluto at 3 Virgo, and Psyche tops it off at 2 Taurus as well.

In the natal chart of Satanic priest Anton LaVey, Amor at 17 Pisces partile trines Pluto at 17 Cancer while widely conjoining Mars at 19 Pisces.

In the natal chart of President John F. Kennedy, Amor at 21 Aries opposes his 19 Libra Ascendant; women found him attractive and his many love affairs were the stuff of legend.

Occultist and magician Aleister Crowley had Amor rising at 8 Leo on his 8 Leo Ascendant; he was a practitioner of sex magic and had many lovers and partners.

Former drummer and heartthrob of the rock group The Beach Boys, Dennis Wilson, had Venus at 22 Capricorn exactly trine Amor in Taurus.

AMPELLA 198

Discovery: June 13, 1879 by Alphonse Borrelly.

Backstory: This name could be the feminine for Ampellus or Ampelos, a satyr and friend of Dionysus, Greek god of wine.

Possible Interpretation: Dionysus, a very lusty, good-time guy, never met a party he didn't like and Ampella may be the same way – guilt by association! May indicate hangers-on or those who attach themselves to celebrities.

Examples: In the natal chart of pop star Taylor Swift, her Moon at 5 Cancer squares Ampella at 5 Libra.

ASTEROIDS OUR COSMIC INFLUENCERS

In the natal chart of Yoko Ono, Japanese artist and wife of musician John Lennon, Venus at 13 Aquarius sextiles Ampella at 13 Sagittarius.

AMPHITRITE 29

Discovery: March 1, 1854 by Albert Marth.

Backstory: She was a Titan sea goddess who was unwillingly married to Poseidon, the God of the Sea. But Poseidon's wandering eye and affection for women disturbed her greatly, and she remained bitter and resentful.

A son Triton was born of this union. He was half man, half fish (a merman) and is often shown blowing a conch shell as trumpeter of the seas.

Possible Interpretation: Her presence in the chart may indicate a tendency toward unfaithful partners, drama involving love triangles, or stressful marriages.

Example: In the natal chart of fraudulent hedge fund manager Bernie Madoff, Sun at 8 Taurus exactly conjoins Amphitrite. His infidelity, misdeeds, and subsequent imprisonment caused extreme duress to his wife and children.

AMUN 3554

Discovery: March 4, 1986 by Eugene and Carolyn Shoemaker.

Backstory: Supreme creator god of Egypt, also known as the snake god or fertility god; his sexual powers were legendary. He was known as the lord of the sky and king of the Egyptian world.

Possible Interpretation: Indicates where one feels powerful, either through physical or sexual attributes; strong leadership abilities and drive; highly developed creativity; the need to control through force of will or sheer guile.

AMYCUS 55576

Discovery: April 8, 2002 by NEAT (Near-Earth Asteroid Tracking) at the Palomar Observatory. Centaur.

Backstory: A Centaur in Greek mythology; son of Poseidon and a skilled boxer. Amicus in Latin means "friend."

Possible Interpretation: May indicate athletic attributes; boxing; the ability to form strong friendships if well aspected, not so if poorly aspected.

Examples: Chicago mob boss Al Capone began his career as a boxing promoter; he had Mars at 29 Capricorn partile conjunct Amycus.

World champion welterweight and middleweight boxer Sugar Ray Leonard has his 7 Virgo Moon in trine to Amycus at 6 Taurus; his Venus at 5 Cancer also sextiles Amycus.

Heavyweight boxing champion Muhammad Ali has Mercury at 13 Aquarius in partile trine to Rhadamanthus, which also formed a sextile to Amycus at 13 Aries.

In the natal chart of heavyweight boxing champion Rocky Marciano, his Moon at 20 Taurus sextiled Amycus at 19 Pisces.

ANAHITA 270

Discovery: October 8, 1887 by Christian Peters.

Backstory: Named after the Avestan divinity Aredvi Sura Anahita, a Persian goddess of war, fertility, and royalty.

Possible Interpretation: May indicate a diva-type, alpha personality; the need to rise above others; a fierce defender of self and family; an empowered woman or personality.

Examples: Supermodel Gisele Bundchen has her Moon at 4 Scorpio in sextile to Andromache at 5 Virgo.

Celebrity Kris Jenner, who had four children by Robert Kardashian and two by Bruce Jenner (now Caitlyn), has Moon at 23 Cancer partile opposite Anahita.

ANDROMACHE 175

Discovery: October 1, 1877 by James Craig Watson.

Backstory: Trojan wife of the warrior Hector who fought and lost his life in the Trojan War, after which she was given in slavery to Neoptolemus, whose wife, Hermione, was childless. Andromache bore him a son, as a result of which jealous Hermione plotted her murder, but she was saved by Peleus.

Possible Interpretation: Indicates the possibility of jealousy and resentment in a third party situation or being trapped in a stressful marriage or relationship. The person may unwittingly find themselves involved in a third-party arrangement through an unfaithful partner.

Example: Supermodel Gisele Bundchen has her Moon at 4 Scorpio conjunct Andromache at 5 Scorpio.

ANGA 3158

Discovery: September 24, 1976 by Nikolai Chernykh.

Backstory: Named for a town in the Russian province of Siberia.

B D SALERNO

Possible Interpretation: As the name sounds like "anger," some astrologers have found that it does connect to individuals with anger management issues, and it is worth looking further into this in cases where this characteristic is present in clients. May also simply reference a connection with Siberia or Russia, its language, history, or culture.

Example: In the natal chart of infamous criminal Charles Manson, Mars at 14 Virgo squares Anga at 15 Sagittarius.

ANGRILLI 18102

Discovery: June 3, 2000 by NEAR (Near Earth Asteroid Research).

Backstory: Named after Francesco Angrilli, influential and well respected Italian aerospace scientist.

Possible Interpretation: Also carries the association with anger or angrily; some astrologers have found that it applies to people with violent tempers and anger management issues.

Example: In the natal chart of actress Nicole Kidman, Venus at 14 Leo squares Angrilli at 15 Taurus.

ANTIGONE 129 [Antigona]

Discovery: February 5, 1873 by Christian Peters.

Backstory: Antigone was the name of a play in three parts by Sophocles which set forth her tragic story. Antigone, princess daughter of Oedipus and Jocasta, sought to bury her dead brother Polinices, but was forbidden from doing so by King Creon. Antigone defied the king's wishes and buried her brother anyway, as the result of which she was then condemned to be buried alive as punishment.

Possible Interpretation: The asteroid relates to family scandal and tragedy; also, trying to do what is right in spite of the consequences. If predominant in a crime chart it may suggest a victim's burial place.

Example: In the natal chart of singer Justin Beiber, Antigone at 29 Gemini partile opposes his Ascendant.

ANTIOPE 90

Discovery: October 1, 1866 by Robert Luther.

Backstory: A lover of Zeus in Greek lore, she became pregnant by him and escaped the wrath of her father Nycteus, who then killed himself out of grief. She gave birth to twin sons and the asteroid may have been so named because it was the first double asteroid to be discovered.

Her uncle Lycus caught up with her and kept her imprisoned, leaving her sons behind; after many years she was able to reunite with them, and they avenged her by killing Lycus and his wife.

Possible Interpretation: As an obviously tragic figure who was unable to control her own fate, Antiope may indicate where we are overpowered by others and forced to give in to certain situations beyond our control; domestic violence.

Example: Princess Grace of Monaco, once known as actress Grace Kelly, had Mars at 25 Scorpio in trine to Antiope at 25 Cancer. Her husband, Prince Rainier, had many mistresses during their unhappy marriage.

ANUBIS 1912

Discovery: September 24, 1960 by Ingrid and C. J. van Houten.

Backstory: Anubis is named after the jackal-headed Egyptian God of the Dead who was the Son of Osiris and brother of Set.

Possible Interpretation: Death or irreversible drastic changes may be a recurring theme in the life; a profession related to death or transformation; criminal activities such as murder.

Examples: In the natal chart of Jeffrey Epstein, the Moon at 10 Aries is partile opposite Anubis.

In the natal chart of Elon Musk, Venus at 19 Gemini partile conjoins Anubis.

In the natal chart of celebrity Sean Combs, a.k.a. "P. Diddy," his Moon at 8 Virgo trines Anubis at 9 Capricorn.

APATHEIA 8273

Discovery: November 29, 1989 by Makio Akiyama and Toshimasa Furuta.

Backstory: It derives from the Greek word for "an immovable soul," which can mean detachment; where we are neutral or indifferent.

Possible Interpretation: May show where we are apathetic to a degree, but also, where we do not embroil ourselves in situations; where we are distant, detached.

Example: In the natal chart of lifestyle expert Martha Stewart, her 25 Sagittarius Moon is exactly conjunct Apatheia.

APHIDAS 121725

Discovery: December 13, 1999 by Carl Hergenrother. Centaur.

Backstory: A member of the Centaur group of asteroids to whom is attributed a mythical story regarding Aphidas' behavior during a battle. He had fallen asleep while drunk and was killed by a spear from Phorbas, a Lapith warrior, while he slept.

ASTEROIDS OUR COSMIC INFLUENCERS

Possible Interpretation: May represent a powerful drive toward securing one's needs and desires; the need to be circumspect regarding one's enemies; carelessness must be avoided at all costs.

Examples: In the natal chart of tennis superstar Serena Williams, the Moon at 20 Virgo is exactly trine to Aphidas at 20 Taurus.

In the natal chart of Scientology founder L. Ron Hubbard, Mercury at 14 Pisces form a partile square to Aphidas.

Junk bond guru Michael Milken, whose scandal rocked Wall Street in the 1980s, has his 8 Virgo Mars partile conjoined to Aphidas, which also trines his 8 Taurus Midheaven.

Dr. Joyce Brothers, popular TV psychologist and author, had Venus at 26 Scorpio exactly conjunct Aphidas. When her career began in the 1950s women in the medical field were not taken very seriously, yet by the 1960s she had become a household name.

APHRODITE 1388 [Venus]

Discovery: September 24, 1935 by Eugène Delporte.

Backstory: The daughter of mighty Zeus, an Olympian, and Tione, a Titan, Aphrodite was a powerful goddess who embodied the ideals of love, beauty, attraction, and sexuality. Her twin brother was Apollo, god of prophecy, music, and leadership.

Possible Interpretation: Where the asteroid appears shows where we embody and express our love and values and where we experience desire and strong attraction; consider Aphrodite a mini-Venus in the horoscope.

Examples: In the natal chart of serial pedophile Jeffrey Epstein, Aphrodite is at 0 Leo is in partile opposition to his Sun at 0 Aquarius and Eros at 1 Aquarius, showing an unhealthy inclination to satisfy his unconventional self-serving and self-gratifying urges. His natal chart comes under scrutiny in a number of places in this reference.

In the natal chart of kidnap/murder victim JonBenet Ramsey, a child beauty pageant contestant, Mercury at 10 Virgo exactly conjoins Aphrodite.

Princess Grace of Monaco, once known as actress Grace Kelly, had 11 Leo at her Midheaven opposite Aphrodite; she was known for her beauty and elegance.

In the natal chart of actor/director/producer Clint Eastwood, Mars at 28 Aries partile conjuncts Aphrodite.

APOLLO 1862

Discovery: April 24, 1932 by Karl Reinmuth, then disappeared from view until 1973.

Backstory: Like Amor, Apollo is not only the name of asteroid 1862 but of an entire belt of asteroids orbiting between Mars and Jupiter, which are approximately 18,232 in number.

There is also a Uranian planet Apollon, which appears in asteroid software but without a number, not to be confused with Apollo 1862.

Apollo is a major Greek deity representing young men coming of age, and is often depicted as a hunter bearing a bow and arrows, or as a musician who plays the lyre. He is the epitome of youthful masculinity.

Possible Interpretations: The asteroid shows where one possesses leadership abilities, be it in sports, physical activities, or music. Apollo also relates to one with prophetic abilities, such as a psychic, or a forward thinker with progressive ideas.

ASTEROIDS OUR COSMIC INFLUENCERS

Apollo was the god whose counsel was sought by the Oracle at Delphi; his messages were spoken through a high priestess (originally Pythia), interpreted by a small group of priests, and the response was then relayed to the questioner.

Apollo may represent an enigmatic leader but not always a well-intentioned one, depending on its aspects.

Examples: In the natal chart of serial pedophile Jeffrey Epstein, Apollo at 29 Leo conjoins fixed star Regulus (he had many powerful connections, including the Royal Family). Apollo partile trines Lust at 29 Sagittarius and squares Lucifer at 28 Scorpio, leaving little room for the imagination as to the nature of these associations.

In the natal chart of SpaceX and Tesla Motors founder Elon Musk, Apollo at 6 Virgo is conjunct his 5 Virgo Moon.

In the natal chart of pop star Taylor Swift, Jupiter at 7 Cancer is partile conjunct Apollo.

In the natal chart of heavyweight boxing champion Muhammad Ali, his 27 Capricorn Sun partile opposes Apollo and conjoins Icarus; he is considered one of the most influential and talented boxers of all time, as well as an outspoken civil rights leader.

Civil rights activist Reverend Martin Luther King, Jr., had Venus at 10 Pisces exactly conjunct Apollo.

In the natal chart of astronaut Neil Armstrong, Apollo at 1 Libra partile trines his Ascendant; Armstrong was a member of the famous Apollo-11 mission to the Moon in July 1969.

APOPHIS 99942

Discovery: June 19, 2004 by astronomers Tucker, Tholen, and Bernardi.

Backstory: There has been much speculation that this asteroid could contact, or pass closely by, the Earth sometime between 2027-2032 (the dates keep changing).

Apophis was the god of Darkness, Chaos, and Destruction, the enemy of sun god Ra, and often depicted as a demon serpent.

Possible Interpretation: It's apparent that this asteroid indicates an individual with extremist tendencies, one with a desire to connect to his shadow self; an interest in death, war, or transformation is indicated; one who has the power to enact great change.

If you look up the glyph for Apophis, you'll see that it covers all the bases: Neptune sits atop the heap with a cross beneath it, the inverse of Venus standing on its head. In some circles Neptune is considered the higher octave of Venus, but here Neptune's companion is reversed, suggesting a darker side to the pair. The base of the symbol has a Scorpionic/Martian-like tail, confirming its no-nonsense intensity. The overall impression from the symbol is suggestive of sacrifice and destruction, yet eventual resurrection.

Examples: The asteroid is prominent in the natal chart of Adolf Hitler: his 6 Capricorn Moon, conjoined by Jupiter at 8 Capricorn, opposes Apophis at 7 Cancer, which itself is conjoined to Chiron at 6 Cancer. To him, healing could only come through total destruction; his "scorched earth" policy, which proposed the total destruction of Germany if it lost the war, exemplifies this.

Apophis at 0 Aquarius exactly conjoins the Sun in the natal chart of Jeffrey Epstein.

In the natal chart of Patsy Ramsey, mother of slain 6-year-old JonBenet, Jupiter at 1 Libra conjoins Apophis at 2 Libra. Both she and her husband have long been suspected of involvement in their daughter's murder.

ASTEROIDS OUR COSMIC INFLUENCERS

In the natal chart of Anton LaVey, founder of the Church of Satan, Apophis at 19 Gemini forms a partile square to Mars at 19 Pisces.

In the natal chart of Elon Musk, founder of SpaceX and Tesla Motors, Apophis at 19 Leo opposes Mars at 20 Aquarius.

In the natal chart of serial rapist/killer/cannibal Jeffrey Dahmer, Apophis at 26 Taurus is conjoined to the malefic fixed star Caput Algol, which signifies brutal violence, decapitation, and fatal injuries to the head and neck. Venus hovers nearby at 22 Taurus although not within the acceptable one degree orb; however, it is a degree of murder. Dahmer's chart hosts a plethora of what I call the "badassteroids," which will be revisited again in these pages.

In the natal chart of British serial killer Rosemary West, her 22 Virgo Moon squares Apophis at 22 Sagittarius. Her partner in crime Fred West, had Venus at 16 Scorpio square Apophis at 16 Leo, showing a liking for violence.

In the natal chart of Italian Prime Minister Aldo Moro, who was kidnapped and murdered by terrorists in 1978, the Moon and Venus, which both occupy 14 Leo, are exactly conjunct Apophis.

Occultist and rocket scientist Jack Parsons, who founded the Jet Propulsion Laboratory, had his 1 Scorpio Mercury partile conjunct Atropos, and conjunct Apophis at 0 Scorpio, forming a trine with his Saturn-Pluto-Charon conjunction in Cancer. Mars at 2 Cancer also fits here. He accidentally blew himself up during an experiment.

ARA 849

Discovery: February 9, 1912 by Sergey Belyavsky.

Backstory: Not much information is available on this asteroid's origin.

Possible Interpretation: Ara will indicate giving and receiving help to or from others depending on the house and sign in which it is placed. When afflicted it can show where support is lacking. The asteroid relates to help and support; caregiving; problems inherited from one's past.

Example: In the natal chart of former President Jimmy Carter, Mars at 25 Aquarius partile trines Ara in Libra.

ARACHNE 407

Discovery: October 13, 1895 by Max Wolf.

Backstory: A skilled weaver of fabrics and tapestries, Arachne proudly challenged goddess Athena to a competition. Pride never went over well with the gods, so Athena punished Arachne for her hubris by turning her into a spider - that way she could forever spin webs to her heart's content.

Possible Interpretations: On a physical level the asteroid may indicate a love of handicraft such as weaving; on a more symbolic level it also relates to one's ability to spin or craft a narrative, whether truthful or not. Also may show a talent that attracts the envy of others.

Examples: I have noted the prominence of Arachne in several crime charts that I worked on where one narrative was presented while another more viable theory was totally passed over or ignored (e.g., the Idaho 4 murders, the Smiley Face killings, the murder of JonBenet Ramsey).

Regarding the Ramsey case, Mars at 27 Virgo exactly trined Arachne at 27 Capricorn at the moment Patsy Ramsey telephoned 911.

In the natal chart of baby kidnap/murder victim Charles Lindbergh, Jr., whose case was once called the "crime of the century," his Sun at 0

ASTEROIDS OUR COSMIC INFLUENCERS

Cancer is partile conjunct Arachne. A great deal of research on this case suggests that an innocent man, Bruno Hauptmann, was convicted and executed for the crime, and that the true story has never been told.

ARAWN 15810

Discovery: May 12, 1994 by Anna Zytkow and Michael Irwin. TNO.

Backstory: Arawn is a Trans-Neptunian object which resides in the Kuiper belt, a quasi-satellite of Pluto, much farther away than the more commonly recognized asteroids that fall between the orbit of Mars and Jupiter.

Named for a Welsh god who ruled the Underworld and saw to the transition of a blessed afterlife. On Samhain, or Halloween, he calls on the souls of both living and dead to join him.

Possible Interpretation: Can show a connection to the British Isles; a fascination with the macabre and supernatural; also representative of magical powers, psychic and mediumistic abilities, or the ability to work with elements of nature.

Examples: In the natal chart of President John F. Kennedy, Arawn at 28 Cancer is conjunct his Saturn at 27 Cancer. He was a strong leader of Irish descent whose death by assassination has fascinated the world since its occurrence in November 1963.

British serial rapist and pedophile Jimmy Savile had Mars at 12 Taurus square Arawn at 13 Leo; he was for many years a leading celebrity and entertainer who hailed from Leeds in northern England.

In the natal chart of Princess Diana, Mercury at 3 Cancer squares Arawn at 2 Libra.

ARDUINA 394

B D SALERNO

Discovery: November 19, 1894 by Alphonse Borrelly.

Backstory: Romano-Celtic goddess-huntress Arduinna, which means "height," she is often depicted riding on the back of a wild boar, and is considered a guardian deity of boars. In this respect she is very similar to the Roman goddess Diana.

Possible Interpretation: A strong individual; one who loves nature, the outdoors, animals, farming; one who does not shy away from responsibility.

Example: In the natal chart of supermodel Cindy Crawford, the 1 Pisces Sun exactly trines Arduina. She lives on a farm and enjoys planting her own vegetables.

ARETE 197

Discovery: May 21, 1879 by Johann Palisa.

Backstory: She was the Greek mother of Nausikaa and wife of Alcinoüs. As Queen of the Phaeacians, she protected Jason and Medea who were journeying to Libya in the face of various dangers.

Possible Interpretation: May show someone who is helpful to others in need or is influential enough to offer protection to others, especially family members.

ARIADNE 43

Discovery: April 15, 1857, by Norman R. Pogson.

Backstory: A princess and daughter of King Minos of Crete. Her story varies as told by ancient writers. She fell in love with Theseus, an Athenian king and son of Poseidon, and helped him find his way to slaying the Minotaur, a Cretan monster. She was eventually abandoned by Theseus and rescued by Dionysus. Zeus gifted her with a crown that became the Corona Borealis.

Possible Interpretations: Her story symbolizes a woman abandoned by one man but rescued by another; also, the complexities in the relationships between families of influence.

Example: In the natal chart of pop star Britney Spears, her 12 Aquarius Moon sextiles Ariadne at 13 Sagittarius.

ARROKOTH 486958

Discovery: June 26, 2016 by Marc Buie. TNO.

Backstory: Named in honor of the Powhatan tribe of the Algonquin nation who inhabited the Tidewater region of Virginia, Maryland, and Delaware. The word means "sky".

Possible Interpretation: The asteroid references knowledge beyond the normal realm; exploration of the beyond; the study of the beginnings of life.

Example: It's interesting that Arrokoth is prominent in the natal chart of my sister, Cheryl Salerno, who lived in the Tidewater area (Virginia Beach, VA) for many years, where she developed and refined her biofield healing practice.

ARSINOË 404

Discovery: June 20, 1895 by Auguste Charlois.

Backstory: Wife of King Ptolemy II and mother of Orestes, a Greek hero. She was posthumously identified as Aphrodite Zephyritis who had as her servant the winged horse Pegasus, an embodiment of the West Wind, Zephyrus.

B D SALERNO

Possible Interpretation: Shows an elevated sense of refinement and grace; distinction; family privilege.

Example: Princess Beatrice of York has Venus at 1 Cancer sextile Arsinöe at 2 Taurus.

ARTEMIS 105

Discovery: October 16, 1868 by James Craig Watson.

Backstory: Known as Diana in Roman mythology, and twin sister to Apollo, she is the warrior princess who was skilled at hunting, strategizing, and negotiations. She also rules the Moon. As goddess of animals and the hunt, she also rules blood sacrifice; her image slowly changed from that of powerful warrior to timid maiden dominated by stepmother Hera.

Possible Interpretation: A bold, assertive approach; preference for working with animals or nature, and knowledgeable in these areas; a love of the hunt, literally or in business; good strategic thinking and negotiating skills; protectiveness.

Example: Pop star/dancer/actress Jennifer Lopez has Saturn at 8 Taurus partile trine Artemis at 8 Virgo.

ASBOLUS 8405

Discovery: Discovered April 5, 1995 by James Scotti and Robert Jedicke. Centaur.

Backstory: Asbolus was a mythical centaur who could read omens in the flight of birds.

Possible Interpretation: Centaurs, being part of primal nature, are very attuned to their surroundings. Asbolus may show someone who is good at sensing omens or signs in the environment, someone very in touch with their more physical, sensual side.

Examples: In the natal chart of occultist and magician Aleister Crowley, Jupiter at 7 Scorpio partile trines Asbolus and Hecate in Cancer.

Russian President Vladimir Putin has Venus at 11 Scorpio in exact trine to Asbolus in Cancer.

ASCLEPIUS 4581

Discovery: March 31, 1989 by Henry Holt and Norman Thomas.

Backstory: The Greek god of healing and medicine, Asclepius was the son of Apollo, originally considered the god of medicine. The centaur Chiron took Asclepius under his wing and trained him in the healing arts. He is represented as the kindly, caring physician, one who worked miracles. One method of healing was by incubation – placing the patient in a sanctuary where he could heal through the guidance of dreams.

Possible Interpretation: May show an interest in medicine or healing or indicate a person who is inclined to fix problems and help others; someone whose presence is healing and comforting; a natural born healer.

Examples: Popular television psychologist Dr. Joyce Brothers (1928-2013), had Asclepius at 26 Libra conjunct her Sun at 27.

In the natal chart of Hindu spiritual leader Paramahansa Yogananda, his 25 Leo Moon opposes Varda at 26 Aquarius.

ASIA 67

Discovery: April 17, 1861 by Norman R. Pogson.

B D SALERNO

Backstory: Refers to both the continent of Asia and a Titan goddess in Greek mythology, and was so named because it was the first asteroid discovered in Asia.

Possible Interpretation: May reference Asia or an interest in travel or studies relating to Asian countries and/or culture.

Example: Yoko Ono, Japanese artist and wife of musician John Lennon, has her 9 Cancer Midheaven opposite Asia at 8 Capricorn.

ASKALAPHUS 4946

Discovery: Discovered January 21, 1988 by Carolyn and Eugene Shoemaker.

Backstory: He was a gardener in the underworld who was turned into an owl by the Greek goddess Demeter.

Possible Interpretation: This asteroid is associated with one being a witness to something or a whistleblower; if poorly placed a gossiper, someone who eavesdrops and tells secrets; spying.

Examples: Charles Taze Russell had his 26 Cancer Mars partile opposite Askalaphus; he was the founder of the Jehovah's Witness religious sect, literally, a "witness."

Expatriate whistleblower Edward Snowden has Mars at 24 Gemini partile conjunct the North Node, in square to Askalaphus at 25 Pisces.

In the natal chart of whistleblower Julian Assange, Venus at 25 Gemini forms a partile square to Askalaphus at 25 Pisces.

Joe Valachi, the first mobster to turn federal witness against the Mafia, had Mercury at 17 Virgo square Askalaphus at 18 Gemini.

ASMODEUS 2174

ASTEROIDS OUR COSMIC INFLUENCERS

Discovery: October 8, 1975 by S.J. Bus and John P. Huchra.

Backstory: Asmodeus is the king of demons according to Jewish legend. He was in love with Sarah and killed her seven successive husbands on their wedding nights. He was defeated by the angel Raphael and lost Sarah to someone else.

Possible Interpretation: This asteroid indicates severe heartbreak, disappointment in love due to jealousy or extreme behavior; possible domestic violence.

Example: Actress Lindsey Lohan has Asmodeus at 27 Libra exactly conjunct her South Node.

ASPASIA 409

Discovery: December 9, 1895 by Auguste Charlois.

Backstory : The intellectual, witty, and charming Aspasia was mistress to Pericles, the Greek war hero, during the Golden Age, and one of many oceanids born to Titans Oceanus and Tethys. She was beloved for her social graces and personality and was adopted as a muse for writing.

Possible Interpretation: Refers to someone who is socially gifted, an inspiration to others, a charming companion.

Example: In the natal chart of Eleanor Roosevelt, wife of former President Franklin D. Roosevelt, Mercury at 2 Libra conjoins Aspasia as 2 Libra.

Eugenie, Princess of York, has her Mercury at 7 Aries partile conjunct Aspasia.

ASTARTE 672

B D SALERNO

Discovery: September 21, 1908 by August Kopff.

Backstory: Sidonian/Phoenician goddess of love, fertility, war, and the evening star. She is largely syncretized with the Roman goddess Aphrodite. She was a consort of Baal Samin and her animal symbol was the sphinx.

Possible Interpretation: The asteroid indicates a strong drive for material comforts and pleasure which may become obsessive; the power to manifest those desires, by persuasion or force; a person of many means.

Example: Tennis champion Martina Navratilova has Saturn at 0 Sagittarius exactly conjunct Astarte; she transformed herself into a champion caliber player through strict diet and exercise regimens.

ASTRAEA 5

Discovery: December 8, 1845 by Karl Ludwig Hencke.

Backstory: Greek virgin goddess of justice and innocence, harmony, good morals and judgment. The fifth largest asteroid to be discovered.

Possible Interpretation: Indicates someone who hangs onto things too long, not knowing when to let go. Can also represent a witness in a crime chart, someone involved in law enforcement, or someone who reveals information.

Examples: In the natal chart of Julian Assange, Astraea at 7 Scorpio exactly conjoins the Moon.

In the natal chart of wrestling champion turned Governor of Minnesota turned conspiracy theorist Jesse "the Body" Ventura, his 22 Cancer Sun exactly opposes Astraea.

ATALANTA 36

ASTEROIDS OUR COSMIC INFLUENCERS

Discovery: October 5, 1855 by H. Goldschmidt.

Backstory: Greek heroine who killed those who lost athletic contests against her. An excellent hunter and runner, she was defeated in a race by Milanion (Hippomenes).

Possible Interpretation: May show where one is athletic or competitive; a commanding physique.

Example: Actress and activist Allison Janney, who is six feet tall, has her Venus at 10 Libra in square to Atalanta at 11 Capricorn.

ATE 111

Discovery: August 14, 1870 by Christian Peters.

Backstory: A daughter of Zeus, she is a minor Greek goddess of rash actions, mischief, ruin, an instigator.

Possible Interpretation: Ate may show where one causes trouble unnecessarily, overreacts to imagined threats, or rushes into difficult situations only to make them worse.

Example: In the natal chart of notorious criminal Charles Manson, his 5 Taurus Ascendant squares Ate at 5 Leo.

ATEN 2062

Discovery: January 7, 1976 by Eleanor Kay Helin.

Backstory: Belongs to the Aten group of asteroids that orbit between Mercury and the Earth. Aten was a supreme creator god of ancient Egypt. His worship evidenced a growing belief in one supreme god. He is never shown as man or animal, but is often depicted as a sun disc with rays extended outward with hands at each end.

Possible Interpretation: May indicate where one shines in a particular area or commands the attention or respect of others.

Examples: Celebrity rapper Jay Z has his Jupiter at 27 Libra partile square Aten at 27 Capricorn.

In the natal chart of film director Steven Spielberg, Mars at 1 Capricorn is conjunct Aten at 0 Capricorn, while Hermes also occupies 1 Capricorn.

ATHOR 161 [also HATHOR]

Discovery: April 19, 1876 by James Craig Watson.

Backstory: She is a major Egyptian mother goddess and goddess of love and sexuality, daughter of sun god Ra and considered mother of all pharaohs. She is associated with erotic dancing which formed part of cult rituals, and is often symbolized as a cow or a snake. She is thought to have been a model for the later Greek goddess Aphrodite.

Possible Interpretation: Indicates a strong desire for the pursuit of physical pleasure and power which can turn destructive; intense love and lust; dancing and music.

Example: Actress Scarlett Johansson has Venus at 10 Capricorn in partile opposition to Athor.

Eugenie, Princess of York, has her 2 Aries Sun trine Athor at 2 Sagittarius.

ATIRA 163693

Discovery: February 11, 2003 by LINEAR Group.

ASTEROIDS OUR COSMIC INFLUENCERS

Backstory: She is the goddess of corn, the Earth, and the Evening Star in the Pawnee Nation of North America, similar to Ceres – see CERES 1.

Possible Interpretation: May represent abundance and prosperity; what sustains and nourishes us; crops and/or farming; land; real estate.

ATLANTIS 1198

Discovery: September 7, 1931 by Karl Reinmuth.

Backstory: Atlantis is often called "the lost continent," as it was a massive land formation that spanned the Atlantic Ocean for over 80,000 years. It was inhabited by people with advanced knowledge of energy and its use in transformation and creation, i.e., the ability to move extremely heavy objects for the purpose of construction - like the pyramids?

Sadly, the Atlantean civilization committed the sin of hubris – they felt invincible and unstoppable, until a massive catastrophe literally sank them to the depths of the ocean. It all played out just like a Greek tragedy in which the gods would humble an arrogant mortal.

Possible Interpretation: Related to the mythical, lost kingdom of Atlantis, this asteroid references excessive pride that comes before a fall, a misguided sense of exclusivity or elitism due to having specialized advanced knowledge not shared with others.

Having higher knowledge, technical know-how, possible connection to previous Atlantean life; past life memories. Could refer to knowledge or use of advanced technology for questionable motives – AI, anyone?

Examples: In the natal chart of wrestling champion turned Governor of Minnesota turned conspiracy theorist Jesse Ventura, his 3 Sagittarius Moon is conjunct Atlantis at 2 Sagittarius.

B D SALERNO

Famous producer of animated cartoons, Walt Disney, had a Jupiter-Saturn conjunction at 15 and 14 Capricorn that opposed Atlantis at 14 Cancer.

In the natal chart of medical intuitive/author/lecturer Caroline Myss, her 21 Sagittarius Ascendant partile trines Atlantis in Leo.

ATROPOS 273

Discovery: March 8, 1888 by Johann Palisa.

Backstory: Asteroid Atropos is one part of the "Moirai" fates (in addition to Klotho & Lachesis). Atropos as a theme has a relationship to endings of all kinds: relationships, business, death, accidents, and illness. She cuts the thread of life that is initially woven by Klotho and measured out by Lachesis, the first two Fates.

Possible Interpretation: Someone who deals with death or endings; organizing the lives or events of others.

Examples: Atropos is prominent in the chart of JonBenet Ramsey's mother, Patsy Ramsey, forming a partile conjunction with her Mars at 12 Aries. Many people still believe she committed the murder of JonBenet, or at the very least, participated in its cover-up; she is undeniably connected to the heinous death of her own child.

Atropos at 22 Cancer sits at the 23 Cancer Midheaven of President John F. Kennedy; his unfortunate assassination and very public death at the hands of powerful enemies will remain a part of his legacy.

Atropos at 29 Aries is at the 28 Aries Midheaven of Elon Musk.

In the natal chart of serial rapist/murderer Randall Woodfield, who claimed over 50 victims, Venus at 14 Capricorn trines Atropos at 15 Virgo.

ASTEROIDS OUR COSMIC INFLUENCERS

In the natal chart of the "Bay Area Rapist" Joseph DeAngelo, Apophis at 26 Aries trines his Sun at 26 Sagittarius and opposes his Venus at 25 Libra (which conjoins his Pecker at 24 Libra).

Occultist and rocket scientist Jack Parsons, who founded the Jet Propulsion Laboratory, had his 1 Scorpio Mercury partile conjunct Atropos, and conjunct Apophis at 0 Scorpio, forming a trine with his Saturn-Pluto-Charon conjunction at 2 Cancer. Mars at 2 Scorpio also fits here. He accidentally blew himself up during an experiment.

Physicist Enrico Fermi, developed of the world's first artificial nuclear reactor, had Mercury at 28 Libra in partile trine to Atropos in Gemini.

ATTILA 1489

Discovery: April 12, 1939 by Gyorgy Kulin.

Backstory: Named after Attila the Hun, the famous barbarian warrior who conquered much of Eurasia.

Possible Interpretation: When afflicted, this asteroid can indicate a kind of ruthless, all-or-nothing brutality to winning or victory; where we may exploit certain people or situations to our benefit.

Examples: Russian President Vladimir Putin has Mercury at 23 Libra trine Attila at 24 Aquarius, and in square to Litva at 24 Capricorn.

Former President George H.W. Bush had his 21 Gemini Sun square Attila at 20 Pisces.

AUGUSTA 254

Discovery: March 31, 1886 by Johann Palisa.

Backstory: Wife of Austrian astronomer von Littrow and known as a champion of women's rights.

Possible Interpretation: May have some literal connection with the name August, Augusta, or the month of August; a supporter of women's rights; feminism.

AURORA 94

Discovery: September 6, 1867 by James Craig Watson.

Backstory: Roman goddess of the dawn, whose Greek counterpart was Eos.

Counterpart Eos was also quite a lusty young woman, which may also resonate in the interpretation of this asteroid. Sensual Aphrodite was quite unhappy about some of Eos' exploits with handsome young men.

Possible Interpretation: Symbolizes an important reckoning or discovery of knowledge; the person's ability to resolve crises, i.e., "it's always darkest before the dawn." A sensual nature.

Example: In the natal chart of pop star Taylor Swift, Mercury at 9 Capricorn is partile conjunct Aurora.

AUSTRIA 136

Discovery: March 18, 1874 by Johann Palisa.

Backstory: Named for the country.

Possible Interpretation: May indicate interest in the country, its history or culture, or travels to that area of Europe.

AUSONIA 63

Discovery: February 10, 1861 by Annibale de Gasparis.

Backstory: Greek name for the lower portion of Italy, also, son of Odysseus and Kallisto.

Possible Interpretation: May reference travels to or studies of Italy, its history and culture.

BACCHUS 2063

Discovery: April 24, 1977 by Charles Kowal.

Backstory: Bacchus, the Roman god of wine and intoxication, and son of Jupiter and Semele, was modeled on the Greek god Dionysus. See DIONYSUS 3671.

Possible Interpretation: If you think wild parties and libations, think Bacchus. He is the rock star's god of sex, drugs, and rock 'n' roll. He is a youth usually depicted with a crown of ivy or grapes bearing a wand as a phallic symbol. Bacchus is often found in event charts where wild parties or celebrations were concerned, also shows a tendency toward alcohol, recreational or prescription drugs; self-indulgence.

Examples: In the natal chart of SpaceX and Tesla Motors founder Elon Musk, Bacchus at 15 Cancer is conjunct his Mercury at 14 Cancer.

Bacchus is prominent in the murder charts of several victims who had either attended bars or parties (some inebriated, some not) and were lured to their deaths by unknown killers.

In the natal chart of notorious drug trafficker Pablo Escobar, Bacchus at 18 Capricorn forms a trine to his Mars-Saturn conjunction in Virgo, at 19 and 18 degrees, respectively.

Former President Bill Clinton has Mars at 6 Libra in square to Dionysus at 6 Cancer. He also has Dionysus' Roman counterpart, Bacchus, at 21 Taurus conjunct his 20 Taurus Moon.

Diplomat, race car driver, and notorious Dominican playboy Porfirio Rubirosa had his Mars at 8 Sagittarius conjunct Bacchus at 7; also, Mars was partile conjunct Medea.

B D SALERNO

In the natal chart of activist migrant worker Cesar Chavez, Bacchus at 1 Aquarius trines his 0 Gemini Midheaven. Here the asteroid is literal; Chavez led a strike of grape harvesters against the Gallo wine corporation.

BAIKONUR 2700

Discovery: December 20, 1976 by Nikolai Chernykh.

Backstory: The first satellite was launched into space from Baikonur, in central Kazakhstan, on October 4, 1957. Baikonur was a Soviet code name for the Baikonur Cosmodrome, the facility from which the satellite was launched.

Possible Interpretation: References space exploration, going way beyond the normal limits to achieve something, taking on a transformative task.

Example: In the natal chart of Russian President Vladimir Putin, his 2 Gemini Moon squares Baikonur at 2 Virgo.

BAVARIA 301

Discovery: November 16, 1890 by Johann Palisa.

Backstory: Region in southern Germany.

Possible Interpretation: Connection to the region geographically or historically; interest in German language, culture, or ancestry.

BEATRIX 83

Discovery: April 26, 1865 by Annibale de Gasparis.

Backstory: The name of Dante's beloved (Beatrice in Italian). One's ideal, an image of the perfect partner; someone worshipped from afar.

ASTEROIDS OUR COSMIC INFLUENCERS

Possible Interpretation: One's concept of an ideal lover or companion, or may simply also reference a woman named Beatrice.

Examples: In the natal chart of supermodel Cindy Crawford, Sun at 1 Pisces sextiles Beatrix at 1 Virgo. As a model she projected an ideal image.

In the natal chart of Beatrice, Princess of York, Mercury at 22 Leo squares Beatrix at 21 Taurus.

BEER 1896

Discovery: October 26, 1971 by Lubos Kohoutek.

Backstory: Named after Arthur Beer, German astronomer.

Possible Interpretation: The asteroid is an example of how the name itself carries into its interpretation. Some astrologers have noted that Beer has been found in strong positions in the chart of heavy drinkers, or those who have had issues with alcohol.

Example: Singer Justin Bieber, who has struggled with drug and alcohol problems, has Sun at 10 Pisces square Beer at 10 Gemini.

In the natal chart of novelist Ernest Hemingway, Mars at 20 Virgo sextiles Beer at 21 Cancer; he had a serious alcohol addiction.

Actress Carrie Fisher had Dionysus at her 25 Taurus Moon in partile trine to Beer at 25 Capricorn; she battled with substance abuse issues during her lifetime, and her Moon was conjunct the difficult fixed star Caput Algol as well.

BELISANA 178

Discovery: November 6, 1877 by Johann Palisa.

B D SALERNO

Backstory: Celtic goddess whose name means "queen of heaven". She is the war goddess among the British Celts, similar in nature to the goddesses Athene or Minerva.

Possible Interpretation: References a strong competitive nature, where one is willing to engage in figurative battle for one's beliefs.

Examples: In the natal chart of German tennis champion Steffi Graf, Mercury at 3 Gemini partile opposes Belisana.

Princess Grace of Monaco, once known as actress Grace Kelly, had her Ascendant at 4 Scorpio partile conjunct Belisana.

President Joe Biden has Mars at 2 Virgo partile conjunct Belisana.

BELLEROPHON 1808

Discovery: September 24, 1960 by C.J. and Ingrid van Houten.

Backstory: Bellerophon is known for taming the spirited horse Pegasus. As grandson of Sisyphus he loved riding, and dreamed of taming wild Pegasus. One night goddess Athena came to him in a dream and gave him a bridle that he awoke with. He easily tamed Pegasus and the two then rode off and defeated the monster Chimaera. But Bellerophon became arrogant and prideful after his victory. Pegasus threw him onto the ground and abandoned him, leaving him to wander as a poor and aimless beggar.

Possible Interpretation: References a bold and aggressive nature, reckless and proud, with possible injury or disability as a result.

Example: In the natal chart of billionaire David Rockefeller, his 14 Capricorn Midheaven partile trines Bellerophon.

BELLONA 28

ASTEROIDS OUR COSMIC INFLUENCERS

Discovery: March 1, 1854 by Robert Luther.

Backstory: Bellona was the Roman Goddess of War. When strongly placed in charts can show where a person is confrontational or willing to fight. Priests who worshipped the deity often engaged in violent dancing and thrashing about with swords, resulting in bloodshed. The cult was initially banned in Rome for this reason.

Possible Interpretation: A bold individual, very confrontational; one who engages in intense activities and overdoes it; a tendency to violence.

Example: In the natal chart of politician Kamala Harris, Jupiter at 24 Taurus squares Bellona at 24 Leo.

BENNU 101955

Discovery: September 11, 1999 by the LINEAR group.

Backstory: The spelling has also been seen as Benu. It is the mythical name of the pet bird of the Egyptian god Osiris. Asteroid Bennu is thought to be evidence of the earliest matter in our universe, consisting of 5% organic materials and containing traces of water, and therefore, may have been inhabited by life many eons ago.

Possible Interpretation: The asteroid may reference beginnings, ancient history, something from the very distant past that still carries its imprint and influence.

BIENOR 54598

Discovery: August 27, 2000 by Deep Ecliptic Survey. TNO Centaur.

Backstory: A mythological centaur.

B D SALERNO

Possible Interpretation: Being half man and half beast, may show a person's strong connection to and love of nature; sensuality; a person with very expansive, generous qualities.

Examples: Iconic actress Marilyn Monroe had her Sun at 10 Gemini partile trine Bienor.

Expatriate whistleblower Edward Snowden has Sun at 29 Gemini exactly opposite Bienor.

Tennis champion Martina Navratilova has her Moon at 12 Aries in partile square to Bienor at 12 Cancer. Bienor also partile conjoins the named asteroid Martina, number 981, not included in these pages.

In the natal chart of Hindu spiritual leader Paramahansa Yogananda, Mars at 5 Aries partile trines Bienor in Leo.

BOHEMIA 371

Discovery: July 16, 1893 by Auguste Charlois.

Backstory: A region in the Czech Republic.

Possible Interpretation: Indicates a tendency to go against the cultural grain, to be "bohemian" or unconventional.

BONONIA 361

Discovery: March 11, 1893 by Auguste Charlois.

Backstory: References Bologna, Italy and also Boulogne-sur-Mer, France.

Possible Interpretation: May indicate an interest in French or Italian studies, history, language, or culture, or travel within those countries.

ASTEROIDS OUR COSMIC INFLUENCERS

Example: Singer/songwriter Lady Gaga has Jupiter at 8 Pisces in exact trine to Bononia in Cancer; she is of Italian descent, with her birth name as Stephanie Germanotta, and recently filmed a movie in Italy about the House of Gucci.

BORASISI 66652

Discovery: September 1999 by Chad Trujillo. TNO Cubewano.

Backstory: Represents a mythical sun in the fictional religion Bokononism, derived from the novel *Cat's Cradle* by science fiction writer Kurt Vonnegut. This asteroid is a cubewano, an object that does not resonate with its surrounding environment, like an outlier or a person who does not march to the same beat as others. Asteroids in the TNO belt tend to indicate a higher or more expansive level of consciousness, much like the outer planets Uranus, Neptune, and Pluto.

Possible Interpretation: May symbolize a maverick, rebel, or forward thinker who breaks convention; someone with an awareness of higher consciousness, the collective, a broad thinker.

Examples: British film director Alfred Hitchcock, the "Master of Suspense," made use of unconventional film angles, themes, and techniques in his groundbreaking work in the film industry. He had Borasisi at 4 Libra partile conjunct Jupiter.

Convicted sex trafficker Ghislaine Maxwell has Borasisi at 0 Capricorn, which is partile conjunct her Mars. She surely marched to the beat of a warped drum.

BRASILIA 293

Discovery: May 20, 1890 by Auguste Charlois.

Backstory: Country of Brazil.

B D SALERNO

Possible Interpretation: May reference travel there, or an interest in its history, culture, or language.

Examples: Brasilia at 17 Taurus is exactly conjunct Mars in the natal chart of Brazilian jazz musician and innovator of the bossa nova genre, Antonio Carlos Jobim.

Brazilian supermodel Gisele Bundchen has Brasilia at 4 Cancer, which squares her 4 Libra Midheaven and trines her Moon at 4 Scorpio.

BURNEY 6235

Discovery: November 14, 1987 by Seiji Ueda and Hiroshi Kaneda.

Backstory: Named after Venetia Katharine Douglas Burney, who suggested the name Pluto for the dwarf planet discovered in 1930 by Clyde Tombaugh.

Possible Interpretation: I hazard a guess that it may reference an astronomer, like its namesake, or a literal connection with fire or arson (burning).

Examples: David Koresh, founder of the Branch Davidian religious sect, had his 13 Aquarius Moon in square to Burney; he and his congregation were destroyed in an explosion of flames during an FBI siege at Waco, Texas in 1993.

Celebrity rapper Jay Z has Mercury at 21 Sagittarius partile conjunct Burney. In 2021 he and wife Beyonce were investigated in relation to the possible arson of their New Orleans mansion.

BYBLIS 199

Discovery: July 9, 1879 by Christian Peters.

Backstory: Named after an incestuous Greek woman, daughter of Miletus, who was in love with her brother Caenus. She was turned into a fountain for her transgressions.

Possible Interpretation: May indicate an unconventional sexual relationship or an interest in them; a player; one who goes outside the boundaries of conventional relationships.

Examples: President of Ukraine Volodymyr Zelenskyy has a Sun-Venus superconjunction in Aquarius partile trine Babylis.

Former President Bill Clinton has Sun at 26 Leo sextile Byblis at 25 Libra.

CALIFORNIA 341

Discovery: September 25, 1892 by Max Wolf.

Backstory: Named after the State of California.

Possible Interpretation: Connection to the state, its government, travel, politics, or residence.

Example: Infamous criminal Charles Manson had his 20 Capricorn Midheaven exactly conjunct California, which is where he settled after many years in and out of prison and where he established the notorious Manson Family cult following.

CALLIOPE 22 [also KALLIOPE]

Discovery: November 16, 1852 by John Russell Hind.

Backstory: The oldest of nine sister muses, Calliope was the Greek muse of epic poetry and the arts, eloquence in speaking, and great storytelling. She was the daughter of Zeus and Mnemosyne, the mother of Orpheus.

B D SALERNO

Possible Interpretation: Indicative of talent in the arts, such as music, writing, acting and narration, as described above, or a teacher or supporter of the fine arts.

Example: Supermodel Cindy Crawford has Mars at 16 Pisces directly conjoining Calliope.

CASANOVA 7328

Discovery: September 20, 1984 by Antonin Mrkos.

Backstory: Named after the famous Italian adventurer Giacomo Casanova, who was a spy, writer, and notorious playboy.

Possible Interpretation: May reference a person of intrigue, someone mysterious, with alluring and seductive qualities; a player in the field of romance.

CERES 1

Discovery: Discovered January 1, 1801 by Giuseppe Piazzi. It was the first and largest asteroid to be discovered and was named after Piazzi's homeland of Sicily, which was primarily an agrarian culture at that time. Dwarf Planet.

Backstory: She is the daughter of Cronos and Rhea, and a consort of Jupiter. Known as "the Great Mother," in Roman mythology, her Greek predecessors include Artemis and Demeter, on whom she was modeled. The word "cereal" originated with Ceres as it comes from wheat and grain crops. She is the Roman goddess of agriculture, fertility, and productivity, and since agriculture provides one's sustenance, her meaning runs on an even deeper psychological level.

Possible Interpretation: Her placement in the horoscope shows how we nourish ourselves and others, how we care for ourselves and others, how we are self-reliant (or not), and also points to psychological issues arising from the lack of such qualities due to poor nurturing in childhood.

If afflicted, may indicate psychological problems relating to poor nurturing in childhood and a tendency to repeat same with one's own children. In a crime chart it could show child abduction or abuse if afflicted, and in the nativity, a poorly placed Ceres could also indicate depression, mental health issues, deep-seated feelings of loss, and family trauma.

Examples: In the natal chart of convicted sex trafficker Ghislaine Maxwell (and cohort of Jeffrey Epstein), Neptune at 12 Scorpio exactly opposes Ceres.

Activist Cesar Chavez, who led many migrant workers' strikes against the big agribusiness companies, had Mars at 20 Gemini in exact opposition to Ceres.

In the natal chart of civil rights leader Reverend Martin Luther King, Jr., the 19 Pisces Moon conjoins G!kúnu'hòmdímà at 20 Pisces. These two bodies also join Ceres at 20 Pisces.

Prince Andrew of Britain has a Venus-Mars conjunction at 28 and 27 Capricorn, respectively, conjunct Ceres at 28, which also forms a trine to Toro at 27 Taurus.

CETO 65489

Discovery: March 22, 2003, by Chad A. Trujillo and Michael Brown. Centaur.

Backstory: Ceto was daughter of Titans Pontus and Gaea and mother to the three Gorgon monsters famous in Greek mythology. One of them was Medusa, who featured an ugly countenance with snakes curling out of her head; those gazing upon her were immediately turned to stone.

Possible Interpretation: Borne of sea gods, she may represent danger from the sea, an affinity with the bizarre, monsters, horror shows or scary movies; nightmares or fears concerning same; monstrous situations.

Examples: In the event chart of the reported kidnapping of JonBenet Ramsey, Mars at 27 Virgo is partile conjunct Ceto.

In the natal chart of pop star Madonna, Jupiter at 26 Libra is exactly opposite Ceto.

Polly Klaas, a tragic child kidnap/murder victim, had Venus at 20 Sagittarius opposite Ceto at 21 Gemini.

Charles Lindbergh Jr., son of world famous aviator Charles Lindbergh, was kidnapped and murdered in March 1932; he had Venus at 4 Leo partile trine Ceto in Aries.

Bobbi Kristina Brown, daughter of singer Whitney Houston, had Ceto at 5 Virgo directly opposite her 5 Pisces Midheaven; she passed away in the same manner as her mother, by accidental drowning in a bathtub.

J. Robert Oppenheimer, "father of the atomic bomb," had his 23 Cancer Moon in partile trine to both Pandora and Ceto in Pisces.

In the natal chart of Hollywood produced Harvey Weinstein, Mercury at 17 Aries partile opposes Ixion, which is also conjunct Ceto at 17 Libra.

CHALDAEA 313

Discovery: August 30, 1891 by Johann Palisa.

ASTEROIDS OUR COSMIC INFLUENCERS

Backstory: The name of a Babylonian nation thought to host the birth of astrology.

Possible Interpretation: May indicate an astrologer or someone who is sympathetic to or involved in metaphysical practices.

Example: Psychic medium Edgar Cayce often channeled astrological information and advice in many of his readings; he had Sun at 28 Pisces conjunct Chaldaea at 27 Pisces.

CHAOS 19521

Discovery: November 19, 1988 by the Deep Ecliptic Survey. TNO.

Backstory: It is a cubewano, a Kuiper belt object that is not in resonance with any planet, so the asteroid is well named. In Greco-Roman mythology Chaos is a male power who, with female power Nyx, represents the empty space that preceded the birth of the cosmos.

Possible Interpretation: Chaos is self-explanatory. If well aspected, may signify someone doing their own thing in their own way, a maverick, an outlier or rebel; otherwise, the potential to cause destruction, to shock, to call attention to extreme situations. Their deeds or influences have the power to affect a generation of individuals.

Examples: In the natal chart of serial rapist/killer/cannibal Jeffrey Dahmer, Chaos at 9 Aries conjoins his 8 Aries Mars and 10 Aries Eros; he was passionately driven by an insane lust to not only control his lovers but to "have" them literally.

French serial strangler Henri Landru had Mars at 4 Capricorn partile conjunct Chaos.

B D SALERNO

British serial killer Fred West had Venus at 16 Scorpio trine Chaos at 17 Pisces; his partner of choice was his wife Rose, who participated in the murders with him.

Infamous British pedophile Jimmy Savile had Mercury at 0 Sagittarius in partile square to Chaos at 0 Pisces.

Mafia hitman-turned-witness Sammy "the Bull" Gravano, has Sun at 21 Pisces exactly conjunct Chaos, which also opposes Crantor; he left dozens of grieving widows and children in his wake.

Migrant worker activist Cesar Chavez, who led many workers' strikes against the big agrichemical companies, had his 0 Gemini Ascendant exactly opposite Chaos.

Hollywood producer and convicted rapist Harvey Weinstein has Sun at 29 Pisces in exact conjunction to Chaos.

CHARIKLO 10199

Discovery: February 15, 1997 by James V. Scotti. Centaur.

Backstory: The asteroid is the largest confirmed centaur in the outer solar system and is named for the centaur wife of Chiron the healer. Her name means "graceful spinner", and it thus symbolizes healing on a soul level, deep conscious awareness, divine protection, and an ability to lessen karma through the practice of grace and forgiveness.

Possible Interpretation: A person with healing abilities, drawn to the healing arts; the ability and/or desire to assist others; a loving and compassionate person.

Examples: In the natal chart of film director Steven Spielberg, Venus at 19 Scorpio is exactly conjunct Chariklo.

ASTEROIDS OUR COSMIC INFLUENCERS

Michael Aquino, Lieutenant Colonel of Psychological Operations, US Army, had his Moon at 13 Cancer exactly conjunct Chariklo; the Moon also trined Juno at 13 Scorpio.

In the natal chart of psychic medium Edgar Cayce, his 12 Taurus Moon exactly trines Chariklo.

CHARYBDIS 388

Discovery: March 7, 1894 by Auguste Charlois.

Backstory: A Greek sea monster in the form of a whirlpool that could suck in an entire boat at one time. Since the meaning relates to consuming, it also indicates eating habits: the sea, with its tides that roll in and out, consumes the beach and all in its way, thus the metaphor for eating.

Possible Interpretation: Charybdis represents an obsessive habit that consumes you or an aspect of your personality that stirs fear in people.

CHILD 4580

Discovery: March 4, 1989 by Eleanor F. Helin.

Backstory: Named after the astronomer Jack B. Child but, like other named asteroids, seems to have its own literal meaning of "child." The asteroid was found in the belly of the constellation Virgo. The asteroid Child issued from the belly of Virgo twice: in January 2019 and September 2023 - so much for the chastity of Virgo the Virgin – she's busted!

Possible Interpretation: One's ability to connect to the inner child; having childlike qualities; understanding experiences from a childlike, innocent point of view. I have Child partile conjunct my Sun and am guilty of occasional goofiness, naivete, and gullibility.

It may also show a love for children, or a desire to be around them, for good or for ill, as the example shows.

Examples: Infamous British pedophile and entertainer Jimmy Savile alone was responsible for some 450 abuses, rapes, molestations, and maltreatment during his long career (at least those are the number of complaints). He had Venus at 2 Scorpio trine Child at 2 Pisces; many of his victims were children in hospitals or care homes. Child is partile conjoined to Juno, showing an idealization of children as desirable partners.

Actress Natalie Wood had Venus at 7 Virgo exactly square Child at 7 Sagittarius; she became a film star before the age of five, by her mother's ambitious design.

CHIMAERA 623

Discovery: January 22, 1907 by K. Loenert.

Backstory: Chimaera was the offspring of Typhon, another monster for whom asteroid 42355 was named. He bore the head of a lion, the body of goat, and a serpent's tail; he was killed by Bellerophon.

Possible Interpretation: This imagery lends itself to interpret the asteroid as someone with unusual amorphous features or someone whose appearance or behavior is strange or unsettling.

Example: Former Iraqi dictator Saddam Hussein had Mercury at 24 Taurus conjunct Chimaera at 23 Taurus.

In the natal chart of celebrity Sean Combs, a.k.a. "P. Diddy," Mars at 29 Capricorn partile squares Typhon in Aries.

CHIRON 2060 [also KIRON]

Discovery: November 1, 1977 by Charles Kowal. Centaur.

Backstory: Chiron was the first centaur discovered and equally the most well-known of the mythical centaurs; arguably Chiron is the most important of all the centaurs. He was the son of Saturn and a sea-nymph.

Early on, he is abandoned by his mother (his first 'wounding'), who is horrified at his half-man, half-human form; he is soon taken to the Sun god Apollo, who teaches Chiron everything he knows about the healing arts. Chiron is later wounded by an arrow from Hercules. The wound never heals despite his healing knowledge, which explains Chiron's well-known nickname as the "Wounded Healer".

Possible Interpretation: Chiron's themes include: the "wounded healer" archetype, learning through suffering, compassion for others' suffering, resistance to pain, healing abilities and transformation through healing.

In crime charts involving murder I believe that Chiron often represents the medical examiners, and when poorly placed there may be some conflict or confusion over the autopsy results.

Example: Famous nurse Clara Barton, who founded the Red Cross after working on the front lines in several military conflicts, had Chiron at 2 Aries conjoined to her 1 Aries Ascendant.

CHRYSEIS 202

Discovery: September 11, 1879 by Christian Peters.

Backstory: A woman who was taken captive by Agamemnon during the Trojan War.

Possible Interpretation: May indicate captivity or abduction, especially in a crime horoscope; being kept against one's will.

Examples: Former Iraqi dictator Saddam Hussein's Sun at 7 Taurus trined Chryseis at 7 Capricorn. Many Iraqi citizens were abducted, imprisoned, tortured, and executed under his reign.

In the natal chart of child beauty pageant contestant and kidnap/murder victim JonBenet Ramsey, Jupiter at 27 Cancer squares Chryseis at 26 Libra.

In the natal chart of actress Ali MacGraw, her 10 Aries Sun exactly conjoins Chryseis. She has recently spoken publicly of her unhappy marriage to actor Steve McQueen.

CHUVASHIA 2670

Discovery: August 14, 1977 by Nikolai Chernykh.

Backstory: Named after the Chuvash Republic of Russia, it is a bright C-complex asteroid.

Possible Interpretation: Little information was available. I venture a guess that its prominence in a horoscope may be related to Russia in some way, or its unusual brightness may signal same in an individual depending on what area of the horoscope is highlighted.

Example: In the natal chart of Russian President Vladimir Putin, Mercury at 23 Libra conjoins Chiuvashia at 24.

CIRCE 34

Discovery: April 6, 1855 by Jean Chacomac.

Backstory: Daughter of Helios and Greek goddess of magic, a witch who turned friends of Odysseus into pigs by feeding them food spiked with moly, a magic herb. Odysseus, with the help of Hermes, was eventually able to reverse the curse and charm her. He ended up spending a year on her island, where she gave birth to their son Telegonus.

Possible Interpretation: References the interest in or practice of magic; interest in psychic phenomena or the supernatural or paranormal; an intrinsic understanding of energies.

Examples: In the natal chart of rock star Courtney Love, former wife of musician Kurt Cobain, the 23 degree Cancer Moon is partile conjunct Circe.

Ukrainian President Zelenskyy has Mercury at 14 Capricorn trine Circe at 15 Virgo.

Celebrity Kim Kardashian has a 26 Virgo Midheaven exactly opposite Circe.

CLEOPATRA 216

Discovery: April 10, 1880 by Johann Palisa.

Backstory: Also spelled as Kleopatra. Queen of Egypt, extremely influential in establishing ties with Rome through her torrid affair with Marc Antony. Responsible for the murder of her brother, she was extremely shrewd and ruthless in achieving her goals, but ended up taking her own life at the early age of 21.

Possible Interpretation: References a strong leader with ambitious goals, maybe too much so, who will seek to obtain their desires at any cost, only to end up badly. May describe someone of royalty or strong political or business influence, a strong leader who is not afraid to be ruthless if it furthers their agenda. Also indicative of great attractiveness or beauty.

Example: Actor Brad Pitt has Mercury at 16 Capricorn in exact square to Kleopatra in Libra.

B D SALERNO

CLYTEMNESTRA 179

[also KLYTEMESTRA]

Discovery: November 11, 1887 by James Craig Watson.

Backstory: Greek queen, unfortunate wife of King Agamemnon and mother of Electra, Orestes and Iphigenia [see ELEKTRA 130].

She is one of the more tragic figures in Greek mythology. Her husband, King Agamemnon, sacrificed their daughter Iphigenia to appease goddess Artemis and ensure a smooth passage of the Greek fleet into the Trojan War. Clytemnestra never forgave him, and when Agamemnon returned from the war she sneakily gave him a hero's welcome, and then bundled him up in a bath wrap and had her lover murder him. Her daughter Electra, loyal to her father, despised her for this. The violent cycle was completed when Orestes killed mother Clytemnestra.

Possible Interpretation: The story references dysfunctional family relations, tension, and intrigue, with domestic violence a strong possibility. It features a kind of reverse Oedipus complex, with the daughter wanting to kill the mother, but for vengeance, as the father is already deceased.

Examples: In the natal chart of Princess Diana, Mars at 1 Virgo conjoins Clytemnestra at 2 Virgo.

Princess Grace of Monaco, once known as actress Grace Kelly, had 11 Leo at her Midheaven partile conjunct Klytemnestra.

COLUMBIA 327

Discovery: March 22, 1892 by Auguste Charlois.

Backstory: Named for explorer Christopher Columbus.

Possible Interpretation: May reference where one is adventurous, desirous of exploration in fields or areas not previously explored.

Example: Robert Oppenheimer, father of the atom bomb, had Sun at 23 Cancer sextile Columbia at 24 Taurus.

Arctic explorer Admiral Richard Byrd had Mars at 1 Capricorn conjunct Columbia at 0 Capricorn.

Famous female aviator Amelia Earhart, who disappeared during a flight on July 2, 1937, and was never seen or heard from again, had Mercury at 12 Leo square Columbia at 13 Scorpio.

CONCORDIA 58

Discovery: March 24, 1860 by Carl Christian Bruhns.

Backstory: The daughter of Zeus and Themis, she is the Roman goddess of peace and harmony.

Possible Interpretation: In the nativity shows where one finds peace of mind and tranquility. If afflicted may show the opposite, where one cannot find or maintain peace of mind for long.

Example: In the natal chart of African-American activist, writer, and educator Booker T. Washington, Mercury at 23 Taurus directly opposes Concordia.

CORDUBA 365

Discovery: March 21, 1893 by Auguste Charlois.

Backstory: Named for the city of Cordoba in Spain.

Possible Interpretation: May indicate an interest in Spanish language, a person of Spanish descent, culture, history, or travel to Spanish-speaking countries.

B D SALERNO

CRANTOR 83982

Discovery: April 12, 2002 by NEAT [Near Earth Asteroid Tracking Laboratory]. Centaur.

Backstory: Crantor, who lived in the 3rd century in Turkey, was a Greek academic philosopher who wrote a seminal work "On Grief". This gave birth to the new genre called "the consolation," offered on the occasion of a death or misfortune, the transitory nature of life.

Possible Interpretation: May reference someone who is involved in some way with grief counseling, such as a psychotherapist, clergy, social worker, writer, or victim's advocate.

Examples: Mafia hitman-turned-witness Sammy "the Bull" Gravano, has Sun at 21 Pisces exactly conjunct Chaos, which also opposes Crantor; he left dozens of grieving widows and children in his wake.

In the natal chart of whistleblower Julian Assange, the 2 Sagittarius Ascendant directly opposes Crantor.

Novelist Stephen King has the Sun at 27 Virgo in direct opposition to Crantor; many of his novels deal with grief and loss.

CUPIDO 763

Discovery: September 25, 1913 by Franz Kaiser.

Backstory: Roman god of love, sex and affection, equivalent to the Greek Eros, he was considered a physically perfect male. [See also EROS 463]. There is also a Uranian planet of the same name, representing the same deity.

Cupido, (a.k.a Cupid), son of Aphrodite, was a god but wed Psyche, a mortal woman, which was a serious no-no in the gods' book. He was an exceptionally beautiful and handsome man, considered too perfect to be gazed upon by a mere mortal, but Psyche could not resist looking at her lover, and got in trouble with Aphrodite as a result.

Possible Interpretation: May show an attachment to physical looks and characteristics over more profound attributes in a person; someone who is in love with love; someone who obsesses over their beloved.

Example: Actress Natalie Wood, whose career began in early childhood and spanned her adolescent and adult years, was beloved by many. With her Moon at 0 Taurus exactly trine Cupido in Virgo and Jupiter exactly opposite Cupido, she had many loves as well.

CYBELE 65

Discovery: March 8, 1861 by Wilhelm Tempel.

Backstory: Regarded as a great mother goddess by both Greeks and Romans, but feared because of her strong primitive instincts and attraction to wild animals. Her rituals were legend, and characterized by wild dancing, thrashing about, and frenzied shouting. She is a prime example of feminine power untamed and unfiltered when unleashed. In view of this legacy Cybele represents a strong feminine archetype in a chart, be it male or female, and where one exhibits the sheer power of one's primal instincts.

Example: Karla Homolka, former wife and killing partner of Canadian serial killer Paul Bernardo, has a partile Sun-Saturn conjunction at 13 Taurus in a partile trine with Cybele at 13 Capricorn; 13 degrees alone is an ominous placement where malefics are concerned. The couple's murders were especially cruel and brutal, including the premeditated rape and murder of Homolka's own teenaged sister.

CYLLARUS 52975

B D SALERNO

Discovery: 12 October 1998 by Nichole Danzl. Centaur.

Backstory: Cyllarus is a mythological centaur who was mortally wounded in battle. His partner, Hylonome, was so aggrieved by the loss that she then took her own life [see HYLONOME 10370].

Possible Interpretation: The asteroid represents where we are exposed to danger, where we take heavy risks whose consequences affect others, where we rush into a situation without giving it sufficient thought; overconfidence.

Examples: Famous nurse Florence Nightingale, who served the wounded and dying during the Crimean War, had Venus at 6 Cancer partile trine Cyllarus at 6 Scorpio.

Popular sitcom actor Matthew Perry had Mars at 12 Sagittarius exactly conjunct Cyllarus. Was foul play involved in his death? A suspect was recently arrested as of this writing. See also ERIS 136199.

In the natal chart of heavyweight boxing champion Muhammad Ali, Venus at 20 Aquarius partile trines Cyllarus at 20 Libra; he fought past his prime, with possible consequences to his health.

Cyllarus at 5 Pisces appears at the 4 Pisces Midheaven of actress Lindsey Lohan.

DAEDALUS 1864

Discovery: March 24, 1971 by Tom Gehrels.

Backstory: He was an inventor, artist, and architect who designed and built a labyrinth for King Minos of Crete, where he ended up imprisoned. He escaped with his father, Icarus, by attaching feathers to his arms with wax and flying away. However, Icarus flew too high in the sky, the hot sun melted the wax on his wings, and he crashed into the ocean. Daedalus instead flew low and made it to Sicily where he built the Temple of Apollo.

Possible Interpretation: In a horoscope Daedalus shows inventiveness, ingenuity, and great skill with engineering, inventing, or scientific pursuits.

Example: In the chart of theoretical physicist Robert Oppenheimer, known as the father of the atomic bomb, Daedalus at 13 Libra is opposite Jupiter at 12 Aries.

DAMOCLES 5335

Discovery: February 18, 1991 by Robert McNaught. Damocloid.

Backstory: Damocles was a colleague of Dionysus and bragged that he could have all the money and power he wanted. As a challenge, Dionysus then gave Damocles everything he wanted to teach him that with great power came great responsibility (a lesson that many modern powerful people have sadly failed to learn).

Possible Interpretation: Pertains to those usually with great powers or responsibilities involving many others, such as military and political leaders, CEOs, investment bankers, etc. With great power and wealth also comes great responsibility, which can impact their personal lives in a negative way. Those with great power inherit are said to have "the sword of Damocles" hanging over their heads – in other words, you wanted it, can you do right by it?

Examples: Singer/songwriter Lady Gaga has Jupiter at 8 Pisces partile conjunct Damocles.

Nurse Clara Barton, founder of the American Red Cross, had Damocles conjunct her North Node at 25 and 26 Aquarius, respectively; she suffered from depression and experienced several breakdowns due to the stress of her responsibilities, but still made important contributions to humanity.

Mega-billionaire Warren Buffett has Damocles at 18 Aquarius exactly trine his 18 Libra Midheaven; with great wealth comes great responsibility, or so they say.

In the natal chart of Prince Andrew of Britain, his 11 Leo Ascendant directly opposes Damocles in Aquarius.

DANAE 61

Discovery: September 9, 1860 by Hermann Goldschmidt.

Backstory: Mother of Perseus in Greek mythology. Her father, Acrisius, tried to keep her a virgin by shutting her away in a cave, but Zeus snuck in and made love to her. As a result of their union she gave birth to Perseus, the hero who killed the Medusa, the horrifying Gorgon of Greek mythological folklore.

Possible Interpretation: May represent where one is sheltered and overprotected but to no avail; being out of control of a situation; vulnerable to control by others.

Example: In the natal chart of pop singer Britney Spears, Danae at 1 Libra sits exactly on her Ascendant and squares her 1 Cancer Midheaven; she has had many legal battles with her father over her fortune.

DAPHNE 41

Discovery: May 22, 1856 by Hermann Goldschmidt.

Backstory: Greek fresh water naiad. She suffered the misfortune of rejecting Apollo's advances, and as punishment was turned into his sacred laurel tree.

ASTEROIDS OUR COSMIC INFLUENCERS

Possible Interpretation: Her story may resonate as romantic rejection followed by retribution.

Example: Actor/director/producer Clint Eastwood's Midheaven at 27 Leo squares Daphne at 26 Scorpio. Some of his many lovers have angrily aired their personal grievances in public.

DAVIDA 511

Discovery: May 30, 1903 by R.S. Dugan.

Backstory: Named after David Peck Todd, an astronomer at Amherst College This large asteroid is far and away the most valued of all asteroids, at approximately 24 quintillion dollars because of its wealth of rare minerals. For the record, a quintillion has 18 zeros, or $24,000,000,000,000,000,000!

Possible Interpretation: I venture a guess that the asteroid may indicate a very resourceful individual or one who achieves great value or wealth; very rare individual qualities; uniqueness of character.

Examples: Singer/songwriter Lady Gaga has Neptune at 5 Capricorn exactly opposite Davida; she has made a fortune from her music, but needs to secure it from loss or dissipation.

Billionaire David Rockefeller had Davida at 26 Leo trine his 26 Aries Ascendant.

DEJANEIRA 158330

Discovery: December 1, 1875 by Alphonse Borrelly.

Backstory: See also NESSUS 7066. Dejaneira, a Caledonian princess, was wife of Heracles (Hercules). One day while out walking they came upon a river; Heracles waded across but Dejaneira could not. Nessus, a lusty centaur, offered to carry her but attempted to rape her midway across; he was killed by a poison arrow from the bow of Heracles. While he lay dying he told Dejaneira to take some of his blood and, if Heracles were ever to stray, the blood would bring him back. The time came when Dejaneira suspected this, so she put some of the blood on Heracles' clothing, thinking the blood was a love potion. But it wasn't – it was instead poisoned, and Heracles suffered so mightily that he lay himself down on a funeral pyre and Zeus claimed his soul for eternity.

Possible Interpretation: The asteroid reliably indicates the presence of some form of manipulation, mistreatment or sexual abuse and violation of physical boundaries. The story of Dejaneira is tragic, and suggests similar misfortune especially when not well aspected. May also suggest insecurity and mistrust in love.

Example: I have also noted this asteroid in crime charts related to sex-based homicides.

DEJOPEJA 184

Discovery: February 28, 1878 by Johann Palisa.

Backstory: A Roman nymph, one of 14 belonging to Juno who was admired for her beauty and perfect physique.

Possible Interpretation: May describe the same in the horoscope.

DEMETER 1108

Discovery: May 31, 1929 by Karl Reinmuth.

Backstory: The asteroid was named after Demeter, the Greek goddess of fruitful soil, vegetation, and agriculture, whose Roman counterpart is Ceres [see CERES 1].

Demeter enjoys a dualistic background; she is the goddess of agriculture and sustenance, yet is also linked to the Underworld where her daughter, Persephone, was tricked to be the wife of Hades [see PERSEPHONE 399]. This search for her daughter caused neglect to the crops, as Demeter was in the Underworld searching for Persephone.

Possible Interpretation: There are layers of complexity to this asteroid's interpretation. She may represent a productive, powerful individual whose work suffers due to family complications, or a parent who becomes engaged in the search for a lost or missing child. Alternate interpretations include matters relating to fertility (farming or personal), issues relating to motherhood, even interest in nutrition and subsistence.

DEPREZ 9795

Discovery: April 14, 1996 by Eric Elst.

Backstory: Named after Brigette Deprez, wife of the astronomer Jozef Denoyelle.

Possible Interpretation: Since the name is similar to depression, it has been found relevant in the charts of persons who experience melancholy, sadness, depression; also indicates those situations or things that cause such feelings.

Examples: In the natal chart of actress Marilyn Monroe, Sun at 10 Gemini forms a square to Deprez at 11 Virgo. She frequently suffered from depression, and heavily used many depressants like alcohol and sleeping pills.

Former President Richard M. Nixon, who was forced to resign over fallout from the Watergate scandal in the early 1970s, had his 17 Virgo Ascendant in exact trine to Deprez in Taurus.

In the natal chart of actress Ali MacGraw, her Moon at 4 Virgo trines Dido at 5 Capricorn. Once married to actor Steve McQueen, she endured repeated abuse and infidelity during their marriage. Deprez at 5 Taurus, signifying a depressed state of mind, fills out a grand trine in this sad situation.

DEUCALION 53311

Discovery: April 18, 1999 by the Deep Ecliptic Survey at Kitt Peak Observatory. TNO.

Backstory: He is the son of Prometheus, father of the human race. When Prometheus foresaw that Zeus was planning to flood the Earth, he counseled Deucalion to build a vessel and set sail with his wife Pyrrha; they were the only mortals to be saved from the catastrophic flood invoked by Zeus. Once on land, they cast rocks over their shoulders, from which sprang up a new, stronger race of humans.

Possible Interpretation: Represents where we may experience divine intervention from a difficult event, an opportunity for renewal through crisis.

Examples: Mercury at 5 Virgo exactly conjoins Deucalion in the natal chart of pop star Madonna.

Pop and R&B singer Whitney Houston had her Mercury at 10 Virgo exactly conjunct Deucalion; she had struggled to rehabilitate herself from drug use.

Nelson Mandela, South Africa's first democractically elected President, had a 20 Scorpio Moon in partile trine to Haumea and enjoyed a spectacular comeback to political life after spending 27 years in prison. Haumea was also joined by Deucalion at 20 Cancer.

DEVIENCE 21419

Discovery: March 20, 1998 by NEAR (Near Earth Asteroid Research).

ASTEROIDS OUR COSMIC INFLUENCERS

Backstory: Named after Stephen Jacob DeVience, a 2005 finalist in the American Intel Science Talent Search.

Possible Interpretation: With its resemblance to the word "deviance," the asteroid has been interpreted as a characteristic of those who deviate from the rules, go against societal norms; a maverick, one who stands out from the rest.

Example: British serial murderer Dennis Nilsen, a gay man who murdered other gay men, had Venus at 13 Scorpio trine Devience at 14 Cancer.

DIANA 78

Discovery: March 15, 1863 by Robert Luther.

Backstory: Known as Artemis by the Greeks; goddess of the hunt, brother to Apollo and daughter of Jupiter. Also goddess of virginity, forests, and the Moon.

Possible Interpretation: She references boldness, athleticism, where one is willing to set forth on a mission to "hunt" for something. A strong feminine personality, Diana is also associated with animals and childbirth.

Examples: Celebrity Oprah Winfrey has both Sun and Venus at 8 Aquarius in exact conjunction to Diana.

Activist Cesar Chavez, who led many migrant farm workers' strikes against the big agribusiness companies, had Moon at 22 Pisces in partile trine to Teharonhiawako at 22 Scorpio; Teharonhiawako was also conjunct Diana.

In the natal chart of Hollywood producer and convicted rapist Harvey Weinstein, Venus at 4 Pisces makes multiple contacts in exact opposition to Dziewanna, Psyche, and Diana, and sextiles Dick at 4 Capricorn, which exactly conjoins Salacia.

In the natal chart of actor Christopher Reeve, who was paralyzed following a fall from a horse, Venus at 27 Libra is conjunct Diana at 28.

DICK 17458

Discovery: October 13, 1990 by Freimut Börngen and Lutz D. Schmadel.

Backstory: Named for German astronomer Wolfgang Dick, but this is one of those many modern asteroids that have acquired dual significance by virtue of their alternate meaning, like BEER 1896 and DEVIENCE 21419, just to name a couple. Some astrologers have made connections with the male phallus, which bears out in their astrological observations.

Possible Interpretation: May reference confidence, masculinity, and also, in crime cases, sexual aberration, aggression, or violence; sex-obsessed or ad"dict"ed. Or, the person may just be one.

Examples: The world's most infamous pedophile, Jimmy Savile, who raped, molested, and abused countless children and young adults (some estimate over 400), had Dick at 9 Capricorn conjunct the South Node.

Former President Bill Clinton has Mercury at 7 Leo square Dick at 8 Scorpio; his sexual misadventures are legend. His Mercury also conjoins Osiris. On a physical level, he suffers from Peyronie's disease, an abnormality of the male organ.

In the natal chart of Hollywood producer and convicted rapist Harvey Weinstein, Venus at 4 Pisces makes multiple contacts in exact opposition to Dziewanna, Psyche, and Diana, and sextiles Dick at 4 Capricorn, which exactly conjoins Salacia.

ASTEROIDS OUR COSMIC INFLUENCERS

DIDO 209

Discovery: October 22, 1879 by Christian Peters.

Backstory: Dido's plight was described in the epic poem *The Aeneid* by Virgil. She was a Carthaginian queen who fell for the Greek hero Aeneas. Initially assaulted by Aeneas, she was then captivated by him and the two became lovers. His voyage was not over, however, and he eventually abandoned her. Devastated, she then took her life.

Possible Interpretation: Represents seduction, possibly rape; the heartbreak of loss or abandonment by one's beloved.

Examples: Laci Peterson, the murdered wife of convicted killer Scott Peterson, had her 27 Aquarius Moon exactly square Dido in Taurus. Thousands mourned her tragic murder, as she was pregnant and Scott had been cheating on her.

In the natal chart of actress Ali MacGraw, her Moon at 4 Virgo trines Dido at 5 Capricorn. Once married to actor Steve McQueen, she endured repeated abuse and infidelity during their marriage. The asteroid Deprez at 5 Taurus, signifying a depressed state of mind, completes a grand trine.

DIKE 99

Discovery: May 28, 1868 by Alphonse Borrelly.

Backstory: A Greek mythical figure, daughter of Zeus and Themis, who represents the spirit of justice, law, and order. She is often depicted as being violated by men, which she reports to the gods so that they may exact retribution; thus, the connection with balancing the scales of justice.

Possible Interpretation: The same may be true of an individual if prominent in the birth chart – the experience of a brutal or unjust act for which justice is sought. And as many asteroids with a dual meaning, this one may also represent gay women, even though it's an unfortunate derogatory term.

Examples: The natal chart of former First Lady Eleanor Roosevelt had Sun at 18 Libra sextile Dike at 18 Leo. She was an outspoken supporter of civil and workers' rights, and she is also thought to have carried on a secret affair with another woman for many years.

Megan Rapinoe, champion women's soccer player, is an activist and a lesbian whose 13 Cancer Sun sextiles Dike at 14 Scorpio.

DIONE 106

Discovery: October 10, 1868 by James Craig Watson.

Backstory: Greek oceanid, a wife of Zeus, and mother of Aphrodite.

Possible Interpretation: May reference an influential woman; a person with notable connections or relations in business, politics or social affairs.

Example: In the natal chart of fraudulent hedge fund manager Bernie Madoff, his 2 Taurus Moon squares Dione at 2 Leo.

DIONYSUS 3671

Discovery: May 27, 1984 by Eugene and Carolyn Shoemaker.

Backstory: The son of Semele, this inimitable Greek god of wine and intoxication is known for his wild festivals of debauchery populated by men wearing animal masks and bearing phallic symbols. In rituals conducted by Dionysian cults huge phalluses were always featured, although Dionysus was linked to sexuality, not fertility.

ASTEROIDS OUR COSMIC INFLUENCERS

Possible Interpretation: The asteroid indicates where we derive hedonistic pleasure, and is prominent in numerous crime charts I have studied in which the unfortunate victims had attended parties or bars and were intoxicated by drinking, drugs, or both. [see BACCHUS 2063]. Self-indulgence.

Examples: Bobbi Kristina Brown, daughter of singer Whitney Houston, had her 22 Cancer Moon in exact conjunction with Dionysus.

Former President Bill Clinton has Mars at 6 Libra in square to Dionysus at 6 Cancer. He also has Dionysus' Roman counterpart, Bacchus, at 21 Taurus conjunct his 20 Taurus Moon.

Diplomat, race car driver, and notorious playboy Porfirio Rubirosa had his South Node at 25 Sagittarius conjunct Lucifer and trine Dionysus at 25 Leo.

Actress Carrie Fisher had Dionysus at 27 Cancer partile opposite her 27 Capricorn Ascendant; she battled with substance abuse issues during her lifetime.

DOLORES 1277

Discovery: April 18, 1933 by Grigory Neujmin.

Backstory: As Dolores means pain and suffering in Spanish, so does the asteroid; also, illness or disability.

Possible Interpretation: As it says, where we may encounter loss, grief or suffering, health problems, or disabilities; giving ourselves over to a higher cause through suffering.

Examples: Former President and Army General Dwight D. Eisenhower had Mercury at 2 Libra in trine to Dolores at 3 Gemini.

B D SALERNO

Attorney/activist Robert F. Kennedy, Jr. has Sun at 27 Capricorn partile opposite Dolores; his family has historically sustained several tragic losses.

DORIS 48

Discovery: September 19, 1857 by Hermann Goldschmidt.

Backstory: A Greek Oceanid and daughter of Titans Oceanus and Tethys. She bore 50 daughter oceanids with Nereus, her brother.

Possible Interpretation: I haven't seen much about Doris but I would venture a guess that she could represent the opportunity to bear many children, or to be extremely productive in creative endeavors.

Example: Former President Jimmy Carter had Mercury at 21 Sagittarius partile opposite Doris.

DUENDE 367943

Discovery: February 23, 2012 by OAM [Astronomical Observatory of Mallorca].

Backstory: A duende is a small dwarf or goblin-like creature in the folklore of Spain, the Philippines, and parts of Latin America. They are childlike beings who can be helpful or mischievous, and are protective of their homes.

Possible Interpretation: Where we exhibit childlike behavior that can also become bothersome or petty.

DZIEWANNA 471143

Discovery: March 13, 2010 by astronomers Andrzej Udalski, Scott Sheppard, Marcin Kubiak, and Chad Trujillo. TNO/SDO.

ASTEROIDS OUR COSMIC INFLUENCERS

Backstory: Named after Devana, Slavic goddess who appears in every way to emulate Diana: she rules wild nature, forests and the hunt. Gold-haired, young and beautiful, she brought the spring and the Moon.

Possible Interpretation: Like Diana, she is a protector of nature and animals, and references an individual with strong earthy connections to nature, physical prowess in hunting or outdoor skills; a fighting spirit; repressed femininity.

Examples: In the natal chart of serial killer Ted Bundy, Dziewanna at 2 Virgo partile squares his Sun in Sagittarius. He took extreme delight in stalking and hunting his female victims before approaching them in a friendly, non-threatening manner.

Singer Whitney Houston had her 10 Virgo Mercury partile conjunct Dziewanna.

In the natal chart of Hollywood producer and convicted rapist Harvey Weinstein, Venus at 4 Pisces makes multiple contacts in exact opposition to Dziewanna, Psyche, and Diana, and sextiles Dick at 4 Capricorn, which exactly conjoins Salacia.

ECHO 60

Discovery: September 14, 1860 by James Ferguson.

Backstory: Echo was a Greek mountain nymph who had the misfortune of falling in love with Narcissus, who would not give her the time of day. Too intimidated to express her feelings she retreated into a shell of self-loathing and self-doubt; she literally shrank to just an echo of herself, having only a voice and no body.

B D SALERNO

Possible Interpretation: In a birth chart she may represent where the person lacks self-confidence or gives away too much of themselves in situations involving unrequited love.

Examples: Child beauty pageant queen JonBenet Ramsey had Mars at 15 Taurus partile conjunct Echo; many expectations to compete and succeed were placed on her.

In the natal chart of Yoko Ono, Japanese artist and wife of musician John Lennon, Moon at 11 Sagittarius partile conjoins Echo.

ECHLECUS 60558

Discovery: March 3, 2000 by Spacewatch at Kitt Peak Observatory. Centaur.

Backstory: Named for a centaur who was killed in battle by a poisonous arrow.

Possible Interpretation: References skill with words in music, speech, and writing; boldness in action, possibly to one's detriment.

Examples: In the natal chart of politician Kamala Harris, Venus at 17 Virgo is partile conjunct Echlecus.

Pop star Taylor Swift has Venus at 1 Aquarius in direct opposition to Echlecus.

Former founder and musician of The Beach Boys, Dennis Wilson had a 22 Leo Ascendant opposed by Echlecus at 22 Aquarius; he struggled with alcohol addiction and accidentally drowned while heavily intoxicated.

EGERIA 13

Discovery: November 2, 1850 by Annibale de Gasparis.

Backstory: Minor Roman water nymph and the wife of the second Roman king, Egeria is a deity of oak trees and was also associated with pregnancy.

Possible Interpretation: Represents fertility and marriage; its glyph is represented by the design of a cup which appears full as a symbol of abundance.

Example: In the natal chart of Kris Jenner, who has six children by Robert Kardashian and Bruce Jenner, Moon at 23 Cancer squares Egeria at 23 Libra.

EIRENE 14 [also IRENE]

Discovery: May 19, 1851 by John Russell Hind.

Backstory: Daughter of Zeus and Themis; Greek goddess of peace.

Possible Interpretation: Indicates where one experiences peace and serenity; having a tranquil or soothing effect on others.

Example: In the natal chart of actress Scarlett Johansson, Mercury at 21 Sagittarius conjoins Eirene at 20; she has a pleasant, well-modulated voice.

ELATUS 31824

Discovery: October 29, 1999 by the Catalina Sky Survey. Centaur.

Backstory: Elatus was a centaur killed in the Trojan War by a poisoned arrow fired by Agamemnon. He was also a seer. The arrow passed through his arm and wounded Chiron in the knee.

Possible Interpretation: The centaurs represent daring and boldness for good or for ill, but they always convey strength and an innate connection to nature. May represent someone who is extra sensitive to their environment, who will fight for their beliefs but feel vulnerable to attack.

Examples: Elatus at 14 Virgo forms a partile square to the Gemini Moon in the birth chart of German tennis star Steffi Graf.

In the natal chart of Super Bowl champion quarterback Tom Brady, Elatus at 17 Libra is exactly conjunct the North Node.

In the natal chart of golf champion Tiger Woods, Mars at 17 Gemini forms a partile trine to Elatus.

ELEKTRA 130 [also ELECTRA]

Discovery: February 17, 1873 by Christian Peters.

Backstory: Greek princess, subject of American playwright Tennessee Williams' play *Mourning Becomes Electra*. Williams' plays featured themes of frustrated and repressed sexuality; this bears keeping in mind when interpreting this asteroid.

Electra's story gave rise to the term "Electra complex," very similar to the "Oedipus complex" in that Electra was very attached to her father; she despised her mother Clytemnestra for the death of her father Agamemnon and swore vengeance against her through her brother Orestes. So the asteroid placement may suggest sexual tension among family members or partners, a desire for vengeance, strong sexual desires which are repressed or thwarted.

Possible Interpretation: The asteroid placement may suggest sexual tension among family members or partners, a desire for vengeance, strong sexual desires which are repressed or thwarted.

ELPIS 59

Discovery: September 12, 1860 by Jean Chacomac.

Backstory: Greek spirit of Hope.

Possible Interpretation: Shows where the person feels hopeful, where they inspire hope in others, or conversely, where they feel utterly lost and hopeless.

Example: In the natal chart of singer/songwriter Lady Gaga, Mars at 0 Capricorn trines Elpis at 0 Taurus.

ENDYMION 342

Discovery: October 17, 1892 by Max Wolf.

Backstory: The first asteroid to be given the name of a male god. A figure in Greek mythology, Endymion was a shepherd who was beloved by Selene, Greek goddess of the Moon.

Possible Interpretation: Endymion represents nurturing a dream, bringing creativity into material form.

Example: In the natal chart of pop star Lady Gaga, her 11 Scorpio Moon forms an exact square to Endymion in Aquarius.

EOS 221

Discovery: January 18, 1882 by Johann Palisa.

Backstory: Greek goddess of the dawn and sunrise. She bore six sons by Aeolos, the storm god son of Poseidon, who became the six winds. According to some sources her tears have been equated with the morning dew.

Possible Interpretation: Indicates new inspiration and creativity, where one is reborn into new circumstances, hopefulness; connection to the weather.

ERATO 62

B D SALERNO

Discovery: September 14, 1860 by Otto Lesser and Wilhelm Julius Foerster.

Backstory: One of the nine Greek muses, presiding over love and love poetry; she also played the lyre.

Possible Interpretation: May show where the person feels romance and how they express it, what inspires them artistically, or an affinity for music and the fine arts.

ERIS 136199

Discovery: June 5, 2005 by Michael A. Brown. Chad Trujillo, and David Rabinowitz. Dwarf Planet.

Backstory: Named for Eris, the Greek goddess of discord and strife, it is the largest dwarf planet known in existence thus far. Eris is the sister of Ares, the war god, and ancient poet Homer wrote of how she delighted in the screams of men engaged in battle. The discoverers nicknamed it in honor of the television woman warrior Xena.

Possible Interpretation: Eris shows where we fight to survive; our combative nature, what we will stand up and fight for.

Examples: In the natal chart of tennis superstar Serena Williams, Mars at 15 Leo is exactly conjunct Eris, while Venus at 16 Scorpio forms a square to it.

Popular sitcom actor Matthew Perry had Eris at 12 Aries in partile trine to Mars in Sagittarius, with the grand trine filled out by Makemake at 12 Leo. His battles with addiction and recovery are well known.

EROS 433

Discovery: August 13, 1898 by Carl Gustav Witt and Auguste Charlois.

ASTEROIDS OUR COSMIC INFLUENCERS

Backstory: Son of Aphrodite and Ares, god of war.

My research indicates that this was the first asteroid to be named for a male god; however, Endymion was discovered six years earlier and was also described as being the first to be named for a male god. In either case, it is worth noting that the asteroids were strictly named for females and female goddesses until the 1890s. By then some 430 asteroids had already been discovered and named after women, both real and mythical.

Possible Interpretation: Represents love, sexuality, desire, passion; doing whatever it takes to obtain the object of one's affection; strong determination toward a goal.

Examples: In the natal chart of serial rapist/killer/cannibal Jeffrey Dahmer, Eros at 10 Aries conjoins his Chaos at 9 Aries and his Mars at 8 Aries.

Olympic champion women's figure skater Peggy Fleming has Eros at 19 Cancer exactly conjunct her Mercury; she was known for her romantic, artistic dance routines on the ice.

In the natal chart of infamous criminal Charles Manson, Jupiter at 27 Scorpio conjoined Eros exactly; he used sex and intimidation to manipulate his followers into committing serious crimes.

ERYNIA 889

Discovery: March 5, 1918 by Max Wolf.

Backstory: Named after the Erinyes, or Three Furies, who relentlessly hounded and tortured mortals until they went mad. The Greeks were even afraid to pronounce their name aloud for fear of stirring their wrath.

B D SALERNO

The Furies were Alecto ("unceasing"), Tisiphone ("avenging murder"), and Megaera ("grudging"), Tisiphone being the most fearsome of the three [Also see TISIPHONE 466].

Possible Interpretation: References traits in a person that may intimidate or even strike fear in others; dealing with threatening situations.

Example: In the natal chart of pop star Taylor Swift, her 21 Sagittarius Sun exactly trines Erynia in Aries. I don't know about her own personality, but she has been harassed by stalkers in the recent past.

ESPERANTO 1421

Discovery: March 18, 1936 by Yrjö Väisälä.

Backstory: Esperanto is a language invented by inventor and writer, Ludwik Lejzer Zamenhof (1859–1917), who used the pseudonym "Doktoro Esperanto". Esperanto was intended to be used as one universal language.

Possible Interpretation: May indicate affinity with languages, a desire to dissolve barriers; unification through adaptation.

EUGENIA 45

Discovery: June 27, 1857 by Hermann Goldschmidt.

Backstory: Named after Empress Eugenia di Montijo, wife of Napoleon III. Thought to be the basis for the famous French novel *The Little Prince*. First asteroid to be named after a real person and not a mythological character, and also the first asteroid to have a moon orbiting it.

Possible Interpretation: Aside from its literal name value, Eugenia may refer to an inspirational person; someone who attracts attention.

ASTEROIDS OUR COSMIC INFLUENCERS

Example: Eugenie, Princess of York and daughter of Prince Andrew, has her North Node at 15 Aquarius conjunct her Venus at 16, which form a trine with Eugenia at 15 Gemini.

EUNOMIA 15

Discovery: July 29, 1851 by Annibale de Gasparis.

Backstory: Minor Greek goddess, born of Zeus and Themis, a supporter of law and order, justice, and legislation.

Possible Interpretation: May be noted in the charts of officers of the law and show where the person is respectful, or disrespectful, of the law, rules, and regulations.

Examples: In the natal chart of President Joe Biden, Mars at 13 Leo trines Eunomia at 13 Sagittarius.

Eunomia at 0 Scorpio trined the 1 Cancer Midheaven of Chief Justice of SCOTUS Antonin Scalia.

EUPHROSYNE 31

Discovery: September 1, 1854 by James Ferguson.

Backstory: One of the Three Greek Charities (Thalia and Aglaea being the other two).

Possible Interpretation: The Three Charities, or Graces as they are also called, were attendants to goddess Aphrodite, so the asteroid in a nativity may relate to providing services for women, such as fashion design, health care, beauty, and related fields; philanthropy, working for charitable causes.

B D SALERNO

Examples: Eleanor Roosevelt, wife of President Franklin D. Roosevelt, was a very popular First Lady who supported and promoted many charities during the Great Depression and World War II.

Celebrity Kris Jenner, mother of the Kardashian/Jenner clan, has Mercury at 25 Libra directly opposite Euphrosyne.

EUROPA 52

Discovery: February 4, 1858 by Hermann Goldschmidt.

Backstory: Greek princess who was abducted by tricky Zeus, who had disguised himself as a bull. Jupiter (Zeus) also has a moon named Europa; apparently she was unable to extract himself from his clutches and remains forever close to him. But not all was lost; she became the first queen of Crete.

Possible Interpretation: May reference a male conquest or kidnapping victim; someone who is tricked into a situation by guile or seduction, but may ultimately make good of the situation.

Example: In the natal chart of kidnap victim Johnny Gosch, Uranus at 8 Libra trine Europa at 9 Aquarius.

EURYDIKE/EURYDICE 75

Discovery: September 22, 1862 by Christian Peters.

Backstory: Wife-to-be of Orpheus and character in one of Greek mythology's most tragic stories. On the day she was to wed Orpheus she stepped on a snake, was bitten, and died. It doesn't get better after that. See ORPHEUS 3361 for the full story.

Possible Interpretation: The asteroid represents sadness in love, tragic loss, the steep price one pays for love, karmic relationships, deep grief over loss of a lover, untimely early death.

ASTEROIDS OUR COSMIC INFLUENCERS

Example: Venus at 24 Taurus trines Eurydike at 24 Virgo in the nativity of Princess Diana.

EURYKLEIA 195

Discovery: April 19, 1879 by Johann Palisa.

Backstory: Greek nurse of Odysseus.

Possible Interpretation: A caregiver.

Examples: Famed nurse Clara Barton, who founded the Red Cross, had Eurykleia at 18 Capricorn in square aspect to her Saturn-Jupiter conjunction at 19 and 20 Aries, respectively.

Florence Nightingale, a renowned nurse who tended to the wounded and dying during the Crimean War, had Venus at 6 Cancer in partile sextile aspect to Eurykleia in Scorpio.

EURYNOME 79

Discovery: September 14, 1863 by James Craig Watson.

Backstory: Greek sea goddess and mother of the Three Graces, who also gave birth to Bellerophon, fathered by Poseidon.

Possible Interpretation: The asteroid may represent one who is lost. She was known for her grace and beauty, and may also indicate those qualities in a horoscope.

Examples: In the natal chart of Princess Grace of Monaco, once known as Grace Kelly the actress, Moon at 21 Pisces exactly opposes Eurynome.

In the natal chart of President Joe Biden, the Sun at 27 Scorpio partile opposes Eurynome; Eurynome is also partile conjunct Melusina. [MELUSINA 373]

B D SALERNO

EUTERPE 27

Discovery: November 8, 1853 by John Russell Hind.

Backstory: Greek muse of music and poetry.

Possible Interpretation: A musician, artist, poet, writer; someone attracted to the fine arts.

Examples: In the natal chart of musician Kurt Cobain, Euterpe at 27 Sagittarius forms a square with the midpoint of his Venus-Saturn conjunction at 26 and 28 Pisces.

In the natal chart of supermodel Cindy Crawford, Mars at 16 Pisces partile opposes Euterpe. She was married to actor Richard Gere for several years.

FAMA 408

Discovery: October 13, 1895 by Max Wolf.

Backstory: Roman goddess of fame.

Possible Interpretation: Indicates area of the life where the individual may gain fame and recognition.

Examples: In the natal chart of actor Brad Pitt, Fama at 10 Cancer forms a t-square between Jupiter at 9 Aries and Mars at 10 Capricorn.

Pop star Taylor Swift has Fama at 9 Capricorn exactly conjunct her Mercury.

FANALE 3478

Discovery: December 14, 1979 by Edward Bowell.

Backstory: Named after Fraser Partington Fanale, an American planetary geologist.

Possible Interpretation: As we have noted, asteroid names seem to resonate to regular words as well as people's names, so I venture a guess that Fanale may also refer to how things are finalized, or how matters tend to turn out; a sense of uncertainty regarding the completion of things.

FANATICA 1589

Discovery: September 13, 1950 by Miguel Itzigsohn.

Backstory: The Latin word "fanaticus" refers to someone who is inspired to be or do something, or someone who is possessed. The details of the particular horoscope will show which is appropriate.

Possible Interpretation: Shows extreme passion about a certain subject, person, or thing; if afflicted, may show a fetish or unhealthy obsession; in a crime chart, could relate to obsession or stalking.

Examples: George Lincoln Rockwell, founder of the American Nazi Party, had Fanatica at 18 Cancer trine his 17 Pisces Sun.

In the natal chart of occultist and magician Aleister Crowley, Fraternitas at 15 Aries conjoins his 16 Aries Midheaven, with Fanatica following close behind at 14 Aries.

FELICITAS 109

Discovery: October 9, 1869 by Christian Peters.

Backstory: Roman goddess of happiness and success.

Possible Interpretation: Shows where the person tends to be the most positive and content with matters of concern in the relevant house and sign; if ill aspected, unwise optimism.

B D SALERNO

Example: Eleanor Roosevelt, wife of President Franklin D. Roosevelt, had her Moon at 19 Cancer in square to Felicitas at 19 Libra. Although they remained married for life, each maintained a secret lover for many years.

FERONIA 72

Discovery: May 29, 1861 by Christian Peters.

Backstory: The name references "feral," an apt term for this Roman goddess of groves, woods, wildlife, and freemen. She is similar to Roman goddess Diana.

Possible Interpretation: In a chart she represents the untamed primal instinct; a love of nature, animals, and the land; agriculture.

Example: In the natal chart of Booker T. Washington, African-American writer, educator, and activist, Uranus at 20 Taurus is conjunct Feronia. He promoted agricultural pursuits, especially gardening, as a way toward gaining self-sufficiency and self-esteem.

FINK 10891

Discovery: August 30, 1977 by OCA-DLR Asteroid Survey.

Backstory: Named after astronomer Uwe Fink; it is also the name given to software that ports Unix programs to Mac OS X systems.

Possible Interpretation: We note time and again how named asteroids have taken on the alternate meaning of the word itself. Here, fink is early Twentieth Century crime slang for a rat, a snitch; "rat fink" was also used. It may refer to a person by the name Fink, which could be extremely helpful if in a crime chart, but it is now also interpreted to mean a snitch or someone who betrays his partners by revealing incriminating information or evidence.

ASTEROIDS OUR COSMIC INFLUENCERS

Examples: Mafia boss John Gotti had Mercury at 26 Scorpio conjunct Fink at 27; his right hand man rolled over on him and he spent the rest of his life in a federal prison. Mercury and Fink were both also partile opposite Astraea in Taurus, which represents witnesses or whistle-blowers.

Sammy "the Bull" Gravano, once the right-hand man of John Gotti who later turned federal witness against the Mafia, has Saturn at 3 Cancer in trine to Fink at 2 Pisces.

FLORA 8

Discovery: October 18, 1847 by John Russell Hind.

Backstory: Roman goddess of gardens, flowers and the springtime.

Possible Interpretation: Represents a love of beauty in nature, as expressed in gardening, floral design, landscaping, hiking, and outdoor activities.

FORTUNA 19

Discovery: August 22, 1852 by John Russell Hind.

Backstory: The Roman goddess of good luck who was especially venerated by women. She is often shown carrying a globe, a rudder, and a cornucopia and is also depicted standing on the wheel of fate.

Possible Interpretation: Shows where one experiences the ups and downs of Lady Fortune; where one excels or fails sometimes due to circumstances beyond one's control.

Example: Famous producer of animated cartoons, Walt Disney, had a Jupiter-Saturn conjunction at 15 and 14 Capricorn that conjoined Fortuna at 15.

B D SALERNO

FRATERNITAS 309

Discovery: April 6, 1891 by Johann Palisa.

Backstory: Latin for fraternity.

Possible Interpretation: Interest or participation in social clubs or fraternities; private groups, secret societies; community outreach programs.

Examples: In the natal chart of occultist and magician Aleister Crowley, Fraternitas at 15 Aries conjoins his 16 Aries Midheaven, with Fanatica following close behind at 14 Aries.

Mega-billionaire Warren Buffett has Fraternitas exact on his 18 Libra Midheaven.

In the crime chart of the Idaho 4, the 10 Scorpio Moon sextiles Fraternitas at 11 Capricorn. Fraternities play an important role in this horrible story.

FREIJA 76

Discovery: October 21, 1862 by Heinrich d'Arrest.

Backstory: Nordic or Germanic goddess of love, beauty, and magic from the Viking period. She was a very popular goddess in Norse mythology and enjoyed many love affairs. In paintings she rode a chariot pulled by two cats and is also shown riding on the back of a bristly boar. She is also associated with death and sorcery and was said to receive half of the souls who died in battle.

Possible Interpretation: May show the individual's most harmonious expression of love and beauty, or if afflicted, its opposite; primal sexuality and power are also possible interpretations. Freija is also associated with Frigg and Freyja who may be iterations of one divine feminine principle.

FRIGGA 77

Discovery: November 12, 1862 by Christian Peters.

Backstory: Wife of Odin and Queen of all Norse gods. She was connected to childbirth, fertility, and protection of the home.

Possible Interpretation: A charismatic feminine force, with regal qualities, or at least, someone with leadership or administrative skills.

GAEA [GAIA] 1184

Discovery: September 5, 1926, by Karl Reinmuth.

Backstory: Also spelled as Gaia or Ge, and also known as Goddess or Mother Earth, she was born of Chaos, and as wife of Uranus gave birth to the original Titans. Having consorted with the Underworld she also created the monster Typhon. She is considered the essence of the earth, and is revered by various cult groups even today.

Possible Interpretation: As the first primordial female, Gaea commands high respect in mythology as raw feminine power, fertility, and strength. She had many mates and bore many children, some without the help of men, including monsters. Shows strong connection to nature, primal drives, a love of the environment and/or environmental causes, an attraction to pre-Christian or pagan beliefs; strong intuitive nature.

GALATEA 74

Discovery: August 29, 1862 by Wilhelm Tempel.

Backstory: A Greek nereid, she was sculpted by Pygmalion into the figure of a beloved ideal woman, but as a statue she could not love Pygmalion in return. In stepped Aphrodite, who then gave life to Galatea so that Pygmalion could marry her - an unusual happy ending.

Possible Interpretation: This asteroid may reflect the desire to manifest one's perfect ideal, to remake someone in one's own image, and on the darker side, to coerce someone into fitting into one's own fantasy projection of them.

The Alfred Hitchcock movie "Vertigo" comes to mind here, in which the main character idealizes a woman so intensely that he subjects her to a complete physical makeover in order to suit his fantasy.

Examples: Child beauty pageant queen JonBenet Ramsey had Galatea at 11 Libra in exact trine to her Aquarius Midheaven.

In the natal chart of Indian spiritual leader and activist Mahatma Gandhi, Sun at 8 Libra exactly conjoins Galatea.

GANYMEDE 1036

Discovery: October 23, 1924 by Walter Baade.

Backstory: Ganymede is also a moon of Jupiter. On January 7, 1610, Galileo Galilei observed three asteroids that turned out to be moons Ganymede, Callisto, and one body that was the combined light from moons Io and Europa.

Reknowned for his unique beauty and physical appeal the child Ganymede was kidnapped by the father of Zeus to be servant to Zeus; he carried cups of water as a servant boy and came to be called The Water Bearer, or Aquarius.

Possible Interpretation: May symbolize child molestation, abduction, or servitude.

Examples: This asteroid was prominent in the crime chart of the infamous kidnapping of newspaper delivery boy Johnny Gosch in September 1982. In Johnny's natal chart, his 24 Capricorn Moon trines Ganymede at 23 Virgo.

In the natal chart of kidnap victim Elizabeth Smart, Ganymede at 2 Libra is conjunct the South Node.

In the natal chart of Italian Prime Minister Aldo Moro, who was kidnapped and murdered in 1978, Neptune at 4 Leo is conjunct Ganymede at 5 Leo.

Polly Klaas, who was kidnapped from her home and later found deceased, had a Jupiter-Saturn conjunction at 9 Libra square Ganymede at 10 Capricorn.

GERMANIA 241

Discovery: September 12, 1884 by Robert Luther.

Backstory: Named for the country of Germany.

Possible Interpretation: May indicate a deep connection to Germany, its history, culture, language, and politics; German ancestral roots.

Example: In the natal chart of Adolf Hitler, asteroid Germania at 21 Aquarius conjoins Uranus at 19 Aquarius. He was the physical embodiment of sociopolitical revolt and upheaval in Twentieth Century Germany.

GILGAMESH 1812

Discovery: September 24, 1960 by C.J. van Houten and Ingrid van Houten-Groeneveld.

Backstory: Gilgamesh was a powerful Mesopotamian hero who embarked on a journey to discover immortality. He was given a plant that would help him achieve this goal, but it was eaten by a snake, and he would never again get a chance to become immortal.

Possible Interpretation: The asteroid suggests one who seeks to overcome natural forces that cannot be overcome, such as old age and death; the drive to become superhuman, resistance to the inevitable stages of life.

Example: In the natal chart of Pope Francis I, Mars at 19 Libra conjoins Gilgamesh at 18.

G!KÚNII'HÒMDÍMÀ 229762

Discovery: October 19, 2007 by Michael E. Brown, Megan Schwamb, and David L. Rabinowitz. TNO.

Backstory: It is pronounced GUH-cool-dee-mah. Named for a lovely aardvark girl in Jul'hoan mythology (southern Africa), who appears as a python or an elephant. She defends her people rigorously and punishes evildoers.

Possible Interpretation: A strong sense of class consciousness; social activist; a righter of social injustices.

Examples: Award-winning actress Allison Janney, who represents many charities and social causes, including animal rights and AIDS patients, has Mercury at 7 Sagittarius exactly trine G!kúnu'hòmdímà.

In the natal chart of wrestling champion turned Governor of Minnesota turned conspiracy theorist Jesse Ventura, his 3 Sagittarius Moon trines G!kun at 3 Aries.

Civil rights activist Jesse Jackson has Venus at 27 Scorpio in partile trine to G!kúnu'hòmdímà.

ASTEROIDS OUR COSMIC INFLUENCERS

In the natal chart of civil rights leader Reverend Martin Luther King, Jr., the 19 Pisces Moon conjoins G!kúnu'hòmdímà at 20 Pisces. These two bodies also join Ceres at 20 Pisces.

GONGGONG 225088

Discovery: July 17, 2007 by Michael E. Brown, Megan Schwamb, and David L. Rabinowitz. TNO/SDO.

Backstory: Named after a Chinese water god, it is one of the "Four Perils" or "Four Criminals" which oppose the "Four Benevolent Animals". The god represents chaos and destruction, but also offers a chance at transformation after the flood waters recede.

Possible Interpretation: Because it is a water god, it may relate mainly to emotional chaos and disruption, after which clarity may ensue; may reference actual physical flooding.

Examples: Wes Craven, famous director of horror movies, had Venus at 0 Leo in direct opposition to Gonggong in Aquarius.

Joe Valachi, the first mobster to turn federal witness against the Mafia, had his Sun at 29 Virgo square Gonggong at 28 Sagittarius.

Actor Denzel Washington has Moon at 9 Aquarius partile conjunct Gonggong.

In the natal chart of Indian activist and spiritual leader Mahatma Gandhi, Gonggong sits atop his 25 Libra Ascendant.

GRIEVE 4451

Discovery: May 19, 1988 by Carolyn Shoemaker.

Backstory: Grief or sorrow.

B D SALERNO

Possible Interpretation: Where a person faces a grievous situation or grieves a loss; involvement with tragic circumstances.

Example: Allen Dulles, longest serving CIA director, (1953-1961) and a bitter enemy of President John F. Kennedy, had Grieve at 17 Gemini opposing his 16 Sagittarius Midheaven and conjunct his 16 Gemini Mars.

GRIMM 6912

Discovery: April 8, 1991 by Eric Elst.

Backstory: Named after Friedrich Melchior or Baron von Grimm, a noted German encyclopedist of the 18th Century.

Possible Interpretation: This asteroid lends itself to options in interpretation. May reference one who keeps meticulous track of information, as if working with books or texts; if associated with Grimm's fairy tales, may indicate a propensity for fairy tales and fantasies; if associated with the state of grimness, a dour or banal outlook.

Example: Celebrity Sean Combs, a.k.a. "P. Diddy," has Venus at 22 Libra partile conjunct Grimm, which describes the state of his affairs during 2024.

In the chart of aviator Amelia Earhart, her 2 Leo Sun partile squares Grimm; she and her aircraft mysteriously went missing during her last flight on July 2, 1937 and neither has ever been found.

GUDRUN 328

Discovery: March 18, 1892 by Max Wolf.

Backstory: Norse wife of Sigurd; the Old Norse name Guðrún means "god's secret lore."

ASTEROIDS OUR COSMIC INFLUENCERS

Possible Interpretation: I have not located much more information on this asteroid; I will venture that it relates to someone interested or involved in Norse mythology, or someone named Gudrun, but I invite the readers to explore their own interpretations.

HAMBURGA 449

Discovery: October 31, 1899 by Max Wolf and Friedrich Schwassmann.

Backstory: Named after German city of Hamburg, which the fast food giant McDonald's attempted to purchase, but this effort was dropped in 1995.

Possible Interpretation: Can literally refer to hamburgers, the city of Hamburg itself, or travel. Should be prominent in the horoscope of Wimpy, cartoon character Popeye's timeless companion.

HARMONIA 40

Discovery: March 31, 1856 by Hermann Goldschmidt.

Backstory: Greek goddess of harmony. Her necklace and robe were taken by warring parties of Thebes, and the necklace was used to bribe one of the leaders not to carry out an attack.

Possible Interpretation: The presence of this may indicate a case of bribery, or literally a necklace or robe, as the case may be, especially in as crime chart. Otherwise it may show a person who is devoted to settling things in a peaceful and harmonious way.

Example: Celebrity Kim Kardashian has her Moon at 28 Pisces conjoining with Harmonia at 27.

HASSE 7478

B D SALERNO

Discovery: July 20, 1993 by Eric Elst.

Backstory: Named after Peter Hasse, a German organist and musician. It also means "hate" in German, giving rise to alternative meaning.

Possible Interpretation: May reference an organist; also, where we feel hatred, what we despise.

Example: Adolf Eichmann, one of Hitler's top Nazi officers who helped organize the "final solution" against the Jews during World War II, had Mars at 1 Taurus in square to Hasse at 0 Aquarius, with Jupiter at 1 Gemini also trining it.

HATSHEPSUT 2436

Discovery: September 24, 1960 by Cornelis van Houten, Ingrid van Houten-Groeneveld and Tom Gehrels.

Backstory: A female Egyptian Pharaoh.

Possible Interpretation: Indicates success, power, and striving to be one of the best against all odds.

Examples: In the nativity of Pope Francis I, Mars at 19 Libra squares Hatshepsut at 20 Capricorn.

In the nativity of champion golfer Tiger Woods, his 7 Capricorn Sun exactly conjoins Hatshepsut.

HAUMEA 136108

Discovery: September 17, 2008 by a team headed by Mike Brown. Dwarf Planet.

Backstory: She is the goddess of childbirth and motherhood in Hawaiian mythology, and mother of many other deities.

ASTEROIDS OUR COSMIC INFLUENCERS

Possible Interpretation: May represent childbirth or motherhood, or rebirth after a symbolic death.

Examples: In the natal chart of Anne Morrow Lindbergh, Haumea at 8 Cancer conjoins the Moon and Mars at 7 Cancer and these three are opposed by Uranus at 6 Capricorn. Her baby son, Charles Lindbergh, Jr., was kidnapped and murdered in March 1932, at one time known as "the crime of the century".

German tennis superstar Steffi Graf has Venus at 7 Taurus in trine to Haumea at 7 Virgo. Sadly, her young daughter Jaz died in a car crash in June 2024.

Casey Anthony, who was acquitted of the murder of her baby daughter Caylee Marie, has Haumea at 23 Virgo in partile opposition to Mercury; she was extremely deceptive in her statements to the police, and has long been suspected of having committed the crime.

Nelson Mandela, South Africa's first democractically elected President, had a 20 Scorpio Moon in partile trine to Haumea and enjoyed a spectacular comeback to political life after spending 27 years in prison. Haumea was also joined by Deucalion at 20 Cancer.

HAZARD 9305

Discovery: October 7, 1986 by Edward Bowell.

Backstory: Named for astronomer Cyril Hazard, who specialized in receiving distant radio transmissions.

Possible Interpretation: Just as it says; something that poses a risk for oneself or others; a quality or thing that becomes dangerous; an obstacle that poses problems; an astronomer or sky scientist; receiving comms or transmissions from the heavens.

Example: Daredevil stunt performer and motorcyclist Evil Knievel had Venus at 2 Sagittarius sextile Hazard at 1 Aquarius. During his career he was involved in several serious accidents, one of which left him unconscious for over a month.

HEBE 6

Discovery: July 1, 1847 by Karl Ludwig Hencke.

Backstory: Daughter of Zeus and Hera, and wife to Heracles, she is a Greek goddess of eternal youth, also called the "Eternal Bloom".

Possible Interpretation: Represents where one feels youthful and energetic, possibly mischievous and spirited; immature.

Examples: Ukrainian President Volodymyr Zelenskyy has 14 Capricorn Mercury partile trine Hebe; he was once an actor who played a clown.

In the natal chart of Prince Andrew of Britain, the Moon at 25 Scorpio is exactly conjunct Hebe.

Hindu spiritual leader Yogananda had his 15 Capricorn Sun conjunct Hebe at 14.

HECUBA 108

Discovery: April 2, 1869 by Robert Luther.

Backstory: Queen as wife of King Priam of Troy who bore him nineteen children, including Hector, Helenus, Troilus, Paris, and Cassandra, whose names also appear in these pages.

After Priam was killed she was taken as a slave by Odysseus. When she found that Polymestor, the man to whom her son Polydorus had been entrusted, had killed him out of greed, she murdered Polymestor and his children. For this she suffered the punishment of being turned into a female dog, and her burial place was thereafter called the "dog's tomb."

Possible Interpretation: Association with a leader or powerful person; the drive to exact retribution and suffer the consequences; betrayal; ruthless behavior.

Examples: With Hecuba being the wife of a king/leader, it is interesting to note the natal chart of Mary Todd Lincoln, wife of the assassinated President Abraham Lincoln. Her Jupiter at 17 Capricorn was conjunct Hecuba at 16 Capricorn. It is interesting to note that Priam of Troy was king during the Trojan War against Greece, while Lincoln was President during the U.S. Civil War between the North and the South (1861-1865).

In the natal chart of infamous criminal Charles Manson, Venus at 18 Scorpio partile squares Hecuba in Aquarius; he was skilled at manipulation and mind control of his "family."

HEKATE 100 [also HECATE]

Discovery: July 11, 1868 by James Craig Watson.

Backstory: Greek goddess of witchcraft, the moon, and witches, with strong standing as a Fury in the Underworld.

Possible Interpretation: She also represents fertility. I have noted the asteroid in charts of those who practiced magic or were skilled in energy manipulation.

Examples: At 7 Cancer in the natal chart of occultist and magician Aleister Crowley, Hecate exactly trines Jupiter at 7 Scorpio and squares the Moon's North Node at 7 Aries.

B D SALERNO

In the natal chart of magician David Copperfield, Hecate at 25 Taurus widely trines his 23 Virgo Sun, which opposes his 26 Pisces Midheaven. Hecate also occupies the empirical degree of the malefic fixed star Caput Algol.

In the natal chart of Dr. Anthony Fauci, Hecate at 5 Gemini forms a partile opposition to Venus at 5 Sagittarius.

In the natal chart of convicted sex trafficker Ghislaine Maxwell, Mercury at 8 Capricorn squares Hecate at 7 Aries.

In the natal chart of David Rockefeller, of the Rockefeller dynasty, Mercury at 26 Taurus (conjunct Algol!) squares Fortuna at 25 Leo, which conjoins Hecate at 25 Leo.

HELENA 101

Discovery: August 15, 1868 by James Craig Watson.

Backstory: In Greek mythology she was considered the most beautiful woman in the world, the "face that launched a thousand ships." The Trojan War was fought over her after she was abducted by Paris, and much bloodshed followed.

Possible Interpretation: May indicate someone of rare beauty, someone engaged in the business of beauty, or someone who generates rivalries, causing dissension and jealousy among others.

Example: In the natal chart of Eugenie, Princess of York, Venus at 16 Aquarius trines Helena at 16 Gemini.

HEPHAISTOS 2212

Discovery: September 27, 1978 by L.I. Chemykh.

ASTEROIDS OUR COSMIC INFLUENCERS

Backstory: The son of Zeus and Hera, he is the god of fire and forging of metals. He was an unattractive god, brutish and malformed, and depending on placement, he represents craftsmanship or some type of physical disability.

Possible Interpretation: A highly skilled individual; a master craftsperson, or someone very adept at their vocation; extreme skill in using tools for transformation; a physical disability.

Examples: In the natal chart of theoretical physicist Stephen Hawking, Hephaistos at 14 Taurus forms a square to Chiron at 13 Leo. He was stricken by ALS (Amyotrophic Lateral Sclerosis, or Lou Gehrig's disease) at an early age and became severely disabled in adulthood. A genius who suffered severe physical limitations, he remained exceptionally productive in teaching, lecturing, and writing.

David Koresh, founder of the Branch Davidian religious sect, had his 24 Leo Sun in partile square to Hephaistos in Taurus; he and his congregation were destroyed in an explosion of flames during an FBI siege at Waco, Texas in 1993.

Enrico Fermi, physicist who developed the world's first artificial nuclear reactor, had his Moon at 27 Aries in opposition to Mercury at 28 Libra, with Hephaistos at 28 Cancer forming a t-square.

Celebrated film director Steven Spielberg's 10 Cancer Ascendant trines Hephaistos at 10 Pisces.

Occultist and rocket scientist Jack Parsons had his 11 Gemini Ascendant in square to Hephaistos at 12 Virgo; he blew himself up in an experiment with explosives at his Jet Propulsion Laboratory.

HERA 103

Discovery: September 7, 1868 by James Craig Watson.

Backstory: Wife and sister of Zeus who was extremely overbearing, jealous, spiteful, and vengeful. She was the fifth most powerful of the Olympian gods and was born of the Titans Rhea and Cronus. Zeus married her through trickery, as he was wont to do when he desired someone.

Possible Interpretation: Hera may represent what makes us jealous or resentful, and also represents marriage and fertility which may become troublesome if the partners are not emotionally mature.

Examples: In the natal chart of politician Kamala Harris, Mercury at 1 Scorpio partile conjoins Hera.

In the chart of Harris' political colleague Hillary Clinton, Saturn at 21 Leo partile trines Hera in Aries.

In the crime horoscope of the Idaho 4 mass murder at the University of Idaho, the 0 Sagittarius Sun exactly conjoins Hera. Possible motives for the murders have included resentment, jealousy, and revenge.

HERACLES 5143 [also HERAKLES]

Discovery: November 7, 1991 by Carolyn Shoemaker.

Backstory: Also commonly known as Hercules in Roman mythology. As a son of Greek gods Zeus and Hera, he is a heroic god of massive strength and stature who completed many difficult tasks known as the Twelve Labors. He was a lover of Dejaneira, whose jealousy led to her poisoning of him. Stricken by extreme pain, he committed suicide according to one legend. See DEJANEIRA 158330.

Possible Interpretation: Shows where one has the strength and power to complete difficult tasks and missions on a physical or purely intellectual level; where one may be vulnerable to a partner's spite.

ASTEROIDS OUR COSMIC INFLUENCERS

Examples: In the natal chart of genius physicist Albert Einstein, his 23 Pisces Sun widely conjoins Heracles at 25 Pisces; he was an intellectual giant of his time and his theories revolutionized the fields of both physics and philosophy.

Tennis great Martina Navratilova has her Moon at 12 Aries partile conjunct Heracles.

Champion ice figure skater Peggy Fleming has her Mars at 6 Libra opposite Heracles at 7 Aries; she won five consecutive U.S. championships and one Olympic gold medal.

Theoretical physicist J. Robert Oppenheimer, "father of the atomic bomb," had Venus in 11 Aries in exact conjunction to Heracles.

In the natal chart of President-elect Donald Trump, Jupiter at 17 Libra opposes Heracles at 18 Aries.

In the natal chart of Russian President Vladimir Putin, his 13 Libra Sun squares Heracles at 13 Capricorn.

HERMES 69230

Discovery: October 28, 1937 by Karl Wilhelm Reinmuth.

Backstory: The asteroid was named because of its swift speed.

Hermes was the Greek messenger of communications, travel, messages, crossroads, and speech. His Roman counterpart was Mercury, a swift, androgynous, often mischievous god whose trademark was speed and rapid change. Relates to all types of information, print, media, or digital, in forms such as books, letters, emails, journals, etc.

Possible Interpretation: May show where one is mentally adept or clever, quick-witted, a smooth talker, a fast learner, a gossiper, a potential troublemaker, depending on its placement and aspects.

Examples: In the natal chart of Ghislaine Maxwell, Mercury at 8 Capricorn is partile conjunct Hermes.

Controversial Youtuber Logan Paul has Mars at 13 Leo in partile trine to both Phaethon and Hermes at 13 Aries.

In the natal chart of film director Steven Spielberg, Mars at 1 Capricorn is conjunct Aten at 0 Capricorn, while Hermes also occupies 1 Capricorn.

HERMIONE 121

Discovery: May 12, 1872 by James Craig Watson.

Backstory: Greek princess and daughter of Menelaus and Helen of Troy.

Possible Interpretation: Asteroid Hermione may indicate being sent or taken away from one's environment, for schooling, custody battles, or other family matters.

HERSILIA 206

Discovery: October 13, 1879 by Christian Peters.

Backstory: Roman wife of Romulus, founder of Rome.

Possible Interpretation: May show a connection to royalty or highly connected people in society or in one's own community.

Example: Eugenie, Princess of York, has Mars at 9 Aquarius partile opposite Hersilia.

HERTHA 135 [also NERTHUS]

Discovery: February 18, 1874 by Christian Peters.

Backstory: Norse goddess, possibly a counterpart to the Viking god Njord. Worshipped by a cult, her statue was carried around in a cart drawn by oxen. The cart, considered sacred, had to be washed and cleaned immediately thereafter, and all that had ministered to it were then slain to ensure its purity.

Possible Interpretation: Hertha relates to fertility, but in view of her backstory, may also indicate someone slightly elevated above the rest who requires special handling and privileges.

Examples: One of Hitler's top Nazi officers, Adolf Eichmann, had Venus at 6 Aries partile opposite Nerthus; he believed the Aryan race to be far superior to all others.

In the natal chart of Princess Grace of Monaco, who was once Grace Kelly the actress, her 21 Pisces Moon is partile conjunct Nerthus.

HESPERIA 69

Discovery: April 29, 1869 by Giovanni Schiaparelli.

Backstory: Classical Greek name for Italy; one of the Hesperides; name meaning "western land". Named for Hesperus, Greek god of the West, as Italy is to the west of Greece.

Possible Interpretation: May show where one tends to end matters, as the sun sets in the West, or an interest in traveling to faraway exotic places.

Example: In the natal chart of spiritual leader and activist Mahatma Gandhi, the Sun at 8 Libra partile opposes Hesperia. A native of India, he began his career as a lawyer in South Africa.

HESTIA 46

Discovery: August 16, 1857 by Norman R. Pogson.

B D SALERNO

Backstory: Greek daughter of Titans, goddess of home, hearth, and family.

Possible Interpretation: Indicates where one feels comfortable, where one operates with ease, situations or places where one feels most in harmony.

HIDALGO 944

Discovery: October 31, 1920 by W. Baade.

Backstory: Named for Mexican hero Miguel Hidalgo y Costilla (1753–1811), who declared Mexico's independence in 1810, precipitating the Mexican War of Independence.

Hidalgo #944 has been recently categorized as an "unusual object," according to the Minor Planet Center website, www.minorplanetcenter.org.

Possible Interpretation: References one's boldness and bravery for supporting a cause, no matter how unpopular, and defending one's beliefs even in the face of extreme adversity.

Examples: Hidalgo at 19 Sagittarius forms a partile opposition to 19 Gemini Venus in the natal chart of Elon Musk.

Princess Diana had Neptune at 8 Scorpio trine Hidalgo at 8 Pisces in her nativity.

In the natal chart of American Nazi Party found George Lincoln Rockwell, his 29 Capricorn Moon partile conjoins Hidalgo.

The 19 Leo Midheaven of Julian Assange forms an exact trine to Hidalgo in Sagittarius.

HINDERER 3404

ASTEROIDS OUR COSMIC INFLUENCERS

Discovery: February 4, 1934 by Karl Wilhelm Reinmuth.

Backstory: Named after German astronomer Fritz Hinderer, but has assumed the literal meaning of hindering or being a hindrance.

Possible Interpretation: Obstructing or interfering; a person or situation that is a nuisance; how and where we encounter them.

Example: Ken Starr, an influential Washington, D.C. attorney who engineered the impeachment of President Bill Clinton, had Hinderer at 21 Gemini conjunct his 20 Gemini North Node.

HIPPOLYTA 10295

Discovery: April 2, 1988 by Carolyn and Eugene Shoemaker.

Backstory: She was the daughter of Ares and warrior queen of the Amazon women, very strong and powerful women who steadfastly refused to marry men. Her father gifted her with a golden girdle to commemorate her superiority over all other Amazon women.

Possible Interpretation: A warrior spirit, whether male or female; power, strength and leadership; may also suggest an inclination toward feminism and women's rights; a strongly independent woman, one not necessarily desirous of marriage.

Example: In the natal chart of tennis champion Martina Navratilova, Mars at 13 Pisces trines Hippolyta at 14 Cancer.

HONORIA 236

Discovery: April 26, 1884 by Johann Palisa.

Backstory: Named after the granddaughter of the Roman Emperor Theodosius I, who conducted negotiations with Attila the Hun, Western Asian conqueror.

B D SALERNO

Possible Interpretation: Shows facility in politics and the conferring of honor by the people.

Example: Eleanor Roosevelt, wife of President Franklin D. Roosevelt, had Venus at 28 Libra in sextile to Honoria at 28 Leo.

HOPI 2938

Discovery: April 5, 1981 by Edward Bowell.

Backstory: This asteroid is named after the Hopi tribe of North America.

Possible Interpretation: It may be an indicator of prejudice or territorial disputes; a strong attachment to a particular culture or tribe.

Example: In the natal chart of Hindu spiritual leader Paramahansa Yogananda, Mars at 5 Aries trines Hopi at 6 Leo.

HORUS 1924

Discovery: September 24, 1960 by Palomar Leiden Laboratory.

Backstory: The Egyptian sky god and one of the most important and well known in the pantheon of Egypt. Son of Osiris and Isis and brother of Seth, with whom he struggled over supremacy for many years. He is often depicted with one eye, the other having been torn out by Seth but later restored by Isis. He is also depicted as a hawk or the head of a falcon with a human form.

Possible Interpretation: Horus is linked to the "light bearer," performer of miracles, connection to cosmic consciousness, interest in development of the third eye, awareness of deeper realms of consciousness.

HOUSE 4950

ASTEROIDS OUR COSMIC INFLUENCERS

Discovery: December 7, 1988.

Backstory: I have not found much information on the background of this asteroid.

Possible Interpretation: May indicate our sense of comfort within ourselves or within a physical place; where we spend a great deal of our time, which may become our symbolic home; interior decorating or real estate; a location where things happen in a crime chart.

Example: In the natal chart of whistleblower Julian Assange, Saturn in 1 Gemini partile squares House; he has spent much of his life in various locations around the world.

Psychic Sylvia Browne had Jupiter at 21 Sagittarius exactly conjunct House.

Psychic trance medium Edgar Cayce also had Jupiter exactly conjunct House at 2 Capricorn.

Television celebrity and lifestyle expert Martha Stewart has Venus at 9 Virgo trine House at 10 Capricorn.

HUYA 38628

Discovery: March 10, 2000 by Quasar Equatorial Survey Team (QUEST). TNO.

Backstory: Named for the South American god of rain.

Possible Interpretation: Rain brings relief and the chance for new growth to dry areas, and so the asteroid may indicate fertility and creativity; bringing new ideas to projects or situations; a rainmaker.

B D SALERNO

Examples: In the natal chart of Ghislaine Maxwell Jupiter at 9 Aquarius is partile conjunct Huya; she was instrumental in assisting Jeffrey Epstein's nefarious honey pot network.

In the natal chart of Brazilian jazz guitarist and innovator Joao Gilberto, Huya is exactly conjunct his 2 Cancer Ascendant.

In the natal chart of mega-billionaire Warren Buffett, Mercury at 3 Libra squares Huya at 3 Cancer.

HYBRIS 430 [also HUBRIS]

Discovery: December 18, 1897 by Auguste Charlois.

Backstory: "Hubris," excessive pride, arrogance or foolishness that leads to downfall.

Possible Interpretation: Depending on placement can show in what areas this excessive pride is experienced.

Examples: In the natal chart of politician Hillary Clinton, Venus at 16 Scorpio partile conjoins Hybris.

In the natal chart of pop star Lady Gaga, Saturn at 9 Sagittarius is exactly conjunct Hybris.

Disgraced former governor Mario Cuomo of New York, who was forced to resign due to fallout from the COVID scandal, has his 14 Sagittarius Sun exactly conjunct Hybris.

HYGEIA 10

Discovery: April 12, 1849 by Annibale de Gasparis.

Backstory: Greek goddess of health and daughter of Asklepios, the god of medicine and healing (Asclepius in Roman mythology).

ASTEROIDS OUR COSMIC INFLUENCERS

Possible Interpretation: One of five sisters associated with healing, she shows where we need to pay attention to our physical, mental, and emotional healing as a preventive measure.

Examples: In the natal chart of President-elect Donald Trump, whose first campaign promised to "drain the swamp," his Sagittarius Moon at 21 partile trines Hygeia in Aries.

In the nativity of Pope Francis, Hygeia is exactly conjunct his 10 Cancer Ascendant.

HYLONOME 10370

Discovery: February 27, 1995 by D.C. Jewitt and J.X. Luu. Centaur.

Backstory: A female Greek centaur, Hylonome was devastated by the death of her partner Cyllarus, who was killed in battle. Unable to deal with the grief, she took her own life.

Possible Interpretation: Represents someone who will go all out for the partner, sacrificing self if necessary; someone who grieves a loss deeply, possibly to the point of suicide; difficulty dealing with heartbreak.

Examples: Singer Whitney Houston, who tragically drowned in a bathtub at the age of 43, had Hylonome at 7 Gemini square her 8 Pisces Ascendant.

Celebrity rapper Jay Z has Mars at 21 Aquarius trine Hylonome at 22 Gemini. He has talked about mental health issues in interviews and in his music.

In the natal chart of actress Ali MacGraw, Mercury at 14 Aries exactly conjoins Hylonome. She has spoken openly of her difficulties during an unhappy marriage to actor Steve McQueen.

B D SALERNO

IANTHE 98

Discovery: April 18, 1868 by Christian Peters.

Backstory: A young maiden who married Iphis, formerly a woman but turned into a man by Isis.

Possible Interpretation: I believe this little-known asteroid represents those with ambiguous sexual leanings; the desire to undergo a sex change; having the physical qualities of the opposite sex.

Examples: Ianthe is prominent in the birth chart of former Olympic champion Bruce Jenner, now known as Caitlyn Jenner, who has a partile grand trine between Sun at 4 Scorpio, Uranus at 4 Cancer, and Ianthe at 4 Pisces.

Kris Jenner, ex-wife of Bruce Jenner (now Caitlyn), has Venus at 29 Scorpio in square to Ianthe at 29 Leo.

Ianthe at 29 Gemini forms an exact trine to Mercury at 29 Libra in the birth chart of tennis champion Serena Williams, whose very tall, muscular build has often been compared to that of a male athlete.

ICARUS 1566

Discovery: June 27, 1949 by Walter Baade.

Backstory: In the famous mythical story of Icarus and Daedalus, Icarus was the son of Daedalus, a skilled builder and engineer. The two were imprisoned in a palace but Daedalus made plans to escape by fashioning wings out of feather and wax so that the two could fly to freedom.

Daedalus warned Icarus not to fly too close to the sun, lest the heat from the sun's ray would melt the wax. Sadly, the youthful Icarus got carried away with the experience of flying, flew too high, and his father's warning was fulfilled when he crashed into the ocean and drowned. Father Daedalus made it safely to an island where he later built a temple dedicated to Apollo.

Possible Interpretation: Accidents, excessive risk, gambles that don't pay off, moving too fast, unsafe driving, poor judgment in high risk activities and sports.

Examples: In the natal chart of Scientology pioneer L. Ron Hubbard, the Sun at 21 Pisces conjoins Icarus at 20 Pisces.

In the natal chart of Jeffrey Epstein, Icarus at 21 Capricorn is partile conjunct his Mercury.

Olympic and world champion boxer Sugar Ray Leonard has Mars at 20 Aquarius conjunct Icarus at 19.

In the natal chart of heavyweight boxing champion Muhammad Ali, his 27 Capricorn Sun partile opposes Apollo and conjoins Icarus; he is considered one of the most influential and talented boxers of all time, but unwisely fought past his prime.

Logan Paul, controversial Youtube celebrity, has Venus at 4 Pisces conjunct Icarus at 5.

INDUSTRIA 389

Discovery: March 8, 1894 by Auguste Charlois.

Backstory: Latin for diligence, hard work.

Possible Interpretation: Where we are most diligent; the application of hard work; areas of life or business that present the opportunity for sustained effort.

B D SALERNO

Examples: Super Bowl champion quarterback Tom Brady has Venus at 1 Cancer in conjunction with Industria at 2 Cancer.

Migrant worker activist Cesar Chavez, who led many workers' strikes against the big agrichemical companies, had his 15 Pisces Mercury square Industria at 15 Gemini.

IO 85

Discovery: September 19, 1855 by Christian Peters.

Backstory: A mortal lover of Zeus (who wasn't?!) Hera, ever-jealous wife of Zeus, turned poor Io into a white cow, but after many incidents with other mythical characters Io wandered off into Egypt, where Zeus restored her to human form. There are a few iterations of Io in the literature, some saying that she eventually became the Egyptian queen Isis.

Possible Interpretation: She may symbolize jealous actions and their consequences, or, redemption in the face of enduring harsh actions by others.

Example: Child beauty pageant queen JonBenet Ramsey had Io at 7 Aquarius partile conjunct her North Node.

IPHIGENIA 112

Discovery: September 19, 1870 by Christian Peters.

Backstory: Greek princess, daughter of Agamemnon and Clytemnestra, who was sacrificed by her father or alternatively according to some sources, was saved by Artemis to become her priestess.

Possible Interpretation: Someone who sacrifices for the family or is heavily relied upon to provide exceptional support for others; a sacrifice.

Example: In the natal chart of JonBenet Ramsey, her 0 Gemini Ascendant partile trines Iphigenia in Libra.

IRIS 7

Discovery: August 3, 1847 by John Russell Hind.

Backstory: Greek goddess of rainbows and messenger to the gods, especially Hera.

Possible Interpretation: Iris shows a depth of feminine intuition; a deep love of the truth, wisdom, and peace; as a rainbow goddess she shows where we may find the silver lining in the cloud; recovery after a crisis.

Examples: Iris at 0 Taurus exactly squares Venus at 0 Leo in the nativity of pop star Madonna.

Bobbi Kristina Brown, daughter of singer Whitney Houston, had Iris at 29 Virgo in square to her 29 Gemini Ascendant.

In the natal chart of golf champion Tiger Woods, his Moon at 22 Sagittarius partile conjoins Iris.

ISIS 42

Discovery: May 23, 1856 by Norman R. Pogson.

Backstory: Egyptian goddess who aids the dead in entering the afterlife. She was also a goddess of mysteries and of fertility, and as both wife and sister to Osiris as well as mother of Horus, Isis was certainly no stranger to family intrigues.

B D SALERNO

Possible Interpretation: She represents hope and the possibility of reunifying disparate elements in situations; reuniting members of a fractured family. Isis may also represent alchemical magical practices, as she reconstructed the body of Osiris from which she bore a child.

Examples: In the natal chart of occultist and magician Aleister Crowley, Isis at 19 Sagittarius forms a partile trine to Uranus at 19 Leo and a sextile to both the 19 Libra Sun and 19 Aquarius Saturn.

In the natal chart of magician Harry Houdini, Isis at 10 Leo precisely trines his Venus at 10 Aries and opposes his Saturn at 11 Aquarius.

In the natal chart of politician Hillary Clinton, Mars at 14 Leo squares Isis at 14 Scorpio.

ISMENE 190

Discovery: September 22, 1878 by Christian Peters.

Backstory: Greek daughter of Oedipus and Jocasta and sister of Princess Antigone, with whom she was often at odds. Her name in Greek means knowledgeable or equal to the moon. The Oedipus family endured many intrigues and tragedies, including the kidnapping of Ismene and Antigone by Creon, King of Thebes; the family was inundated with drama.

Possible Interpretation: May reference complex and tense family relationships; passivity and complacency in the face of difficulties.

Example: Infamous criminal Charles Manson's 20 Capricorn Midheaven exactly opposed Ismene.

ITOKAWA 25143

Discovery: Sept. 26, 1998 by the Lincoln Laboratory Near-Earth Asteroid Research Team. TNO.

ASTEROIDS OUR COSMIC INFLUENCERS

Backstory: First asteroid to have its samples brought to earth for analysis in 2005, it was named after Japanese aerospace engineer Hideo Itokawa, who is regarded as the father of Japanese rocketry. Evidence of water and organic minerals have been detected on its surface, leading to the belief that it was once inhabited by living organisms.

Possible Interpretation: Not much information was available. I venture a literal guess that the asteroid may reference an interest in astronomy, aerospace engineering, or science, possibly with a connection to Japan or eastern Asia, and I also note reference to finding oneself in a situation that is hard to get out of; defeat.

Examples: Former drummer of The Beach Boys, Dennis Wilson, had Mars at 6 Sagittarius conjunct Itokawa at 5 and also Apollo at 5; the band established its own unique style of music but struggled with addiction and internal conflicts.

In the natal chart of long-time FBI director J. Edgar Hoover, Mars at 0 Taurus squares Itokawa at 0 Aquarius. His posthumous reputation has been tainted by revelations of abuse of power, blackmail, and corruption.

IXION 28978

Discovery: May 22, 2001 by a team of American astronomers at the Cerro Tololo Inter-American Observatory in Chile. TNO.

Backstory: A mythical king of Lapith, in Thessaly, he broke the law by impulsively killing his father-in-law but Zeus pardoned him and allowed him on Mount Olympus as a guest. Ixion repaid Zeus' kindness by attempting to seduce Zeus' wife, Hera. To top it all off, Ixion died without remorse for his actions. He was bound to a spinning wheel for all eternity, but that was later transferred to Tartarus.

Possible Interpretation: References taking matters too far into one's own hands without regard for social norms; lack of gratitude for kindness; getting a second chance but blowing it.

Examples: In the natal chart of politician Kamala Harris, the Sun at 27 Libra conjoins Ixion at 28 Libra, while Saturn at 28 Aquarius trines it.

Iconic actress Marilyn Monroe had Mars at 20 Pisces in direct opposition to Ixion. She was irate over being cast aside by the Kennedy brothers and threatened to expose their affair, which had catastrophic repercussions for her.

In the natal chart of Hollywood produced Harvey Weinstein, Mercury at 17 Aries partile opposes Ixion, which is also conjunct Ceto at 17 Libra.

In the natal chart of French President Emmanuel Macron, Mars at 11 Leo squares Ixion at 12 Scorpio. During his second term his government is currently in chaos following a vote of no confidence.

JOCASTA 899 [also JOKASTE]

Discovery: August 3, 1918 by Maximilian Wolf.

Backstory: Jocasta was the mother of Oedipus, who slew his father in order to marry her, then later was so remorseful that he blinded himself. She was also the mother of Antigone and Ismene, daughters who endured their own physical and psychological traumas. [see ANTIGONE 129 and ISMENE 190]

Possible Interpretation: May reference danger through a partner or beloved; trauma or drama through a dysfunctional family; suffering through the behavior of others, including one's own children.

ASTEROIDS OUR COSMIC INFLUENCERS

Examples: Pop singer Britney Spears has her Ascendant at 2 Libra sextile Jocasta at 1 Sagittarius. She has faced considerable challenges within her family regarding the conservatorship of her finances.

In the natal chart of actress Ali MacGraw, Mars at 6 Capricorn trines Jokaste at 7 Taurus; she underwent a bitter divorce from husband Steve McQueen, claiming abuse and infidelity.

JOHANNA 127

Discovery: November 5, 1872 by Paul and Prosper Henry.

Backstory: This asteroid is thought to be named after Joan of Arc (see also LIBERATRIX 125].

Possible Interpretation: A savior or one who sacrifices for a cause; someone who places their beliefs and ideologies on a higher plane than most.

Example: Queen Christina of the Netherlands has a 28 Scorpio Ascendant in trine to Johanna at 29 Cancer.

JUEWA 139

Discovery: October 10, 1874 by James Craig Watson.

Backstory: Chinese for "Star of China's Fortune."

Possible Interpretation: Indicates connection to China, its politics, its history, or travel there.

Example: In the natal chart of former Communist leader Mao Tse-tung, Juewa is found at 15 Taurus opposite Uranus at 15 Scorpio and asteroid Tantalus at 14 Scorpio. He just had to have that power at whatever the cost.

JUNO 3

B D SALERNO

Discovery: September 1, 1804 by Karl Harding; one of the 20 largest asteroids.

Backstory: Hera was the highly strung wife of Zeus who was known for a nasty temper and fits of jealousy; she represented female sexuality and the three life phases of women – as maiden, mother, and widow.

When Hera wed Zeus she became Juno, wedded to Jupiter [see also HERA 103]. She was the symbol of wifely fidelity and marital commitment; thus, being wed to philandering Jupiter, she was miserable and frustrated in her marriage, and experienced multiple clashes with the many paramours of her husband, many of which she engineered herself.

Possible Interpretation: Shows how we relate and connect in relationships - or don't; what are our tendencies and needs in intimate connections; our ideal concept of a partner.

Examples: Michael Aquino, Lieutenant Colonel of Psychological Operations, US Army, had his Moon at 13 Cancer exactly conjunct Chariklo; the Moon also trined Juno at 13 Scorpio.

In the natal chart of supermodel Cindy Crawford, the 22 Cancer Ascendant exactly trines both Mnemosyne and Juno at 22 Pisces.

Rock 'n' roll king Elvis Presley had Juno conjunct his North Node at 1 Aquarius; as the first rock 'n' roll idol, he was destined to project an ideal image to the public.

KAGARA 469705

Discovery: March 11, 2005 by Marc Buie. TNO.

Backstory: Kagara is a god in San mythology associated with lightning; the San are a tribe of bushmen in the Kalahari region of

South Africa who are among the world's oldest indigenous living peoples.

Possible Interpretation: Information not readily available; I hazard a guess that the asteroid may relate to brilliance, or a greater connection to universal consciousness; also, the tendency to receive quick "strikes" of ideas seemingly from nowhere.

Examples: Hedge fund manager Bernie Madoff, who scammed dozens of investors into thinking they had struck gold with his fraudulent investment schemes, had his 2 Taurus Moon partile conjunct Kagara.

Joe Valachi, the first mobster to turn federal witness against the Mafia, had Jupiter at 28 Aries conjunct Kagara at 29. Though determined to never rat out his associates, he immediately changed course once he learned that a contract had been put out on his life.

KALLISTO 204 [also CALLISTO]

Discovery: October 8, 1879 by Johann Palisa.

Backstory: This is a sad story of a nymph of goddess Diana who swore celibacy as part of a cult dedicated to her, but Kallisto was raped, which resulted in her disgrace and fell out of favor with her leader. Diana turned her into a bear, which still managed to give birth to a human, and Callisto was then sent to the heavens as the Great Bear of the Ursa Major constellation.

Possible Interpretation: Kallisto refers to social grace, charm, and beauty, but also references an unwanted and consequential seduction.

Example: Yoko Ono, Japanese artist and wife of musician John Lennon, has Libra rising at 8 degrees in exact trine to Kallisto in Gemini; note that the 8 Libra degree also conjoins the fixed star Vindemiatrix, which represents a widow.

B D SALERNO

KALYPSO 53

Discovery: April 4, 1858 by Robert Luther.

Backstory: Named after a sea nymph, daughter of a Titan and also shares her name with Calypso, a moon of Saturn. There is a mythical Calypso, spelled with a 'c', who was daughter of Atlas; she detained Odysseus on her island of Ogygia during his travels.

Possible Interpretation: There is not much information on Kalypso but I would venture a guess that it may show a connection with song, dance, or Caribbean culture.

Examples: In the natal chart of Jamaican reggae singer Bob Marley, Kalypso at 18 Aquarius trines his 17 Aquarius Sun. While his was not specifically calypso music, its origin was also Latin American.

In the natal chart of Latina singer/dancer Carmen Miranda, who popularized the Brazilian samba, Kalypso at 24 Libra trines her Mercury at 24 Aquarius and forms a grand trine with Pluto at 23 Gemini.

Brazilian jazz musician and innovator Antonio Carlos Jobim had Kalypso at 26 Sagittarius in partile trine to Neptune in Leo and square to Uranus in 26 Pisces; Sag, Neptune, Leo, and Pisces all relate to music and the performing arts, and Uranus rules the innovator, as he was the creator of a new jazz genre.

KARMA 3811

Discovery: October 13, 1953 by Sylvain Arend and Liisi Oterma.

Backstory: This asteroid is exactly as it sounds, dealing with karmic relationships, events, or situations that go back lifetimes.

Possible Interpretation: May indicate the nature of a person's karma in a particular area depending on how it is aspected; a person's connectedness to ancestral roots and their influences.

Examples: In the natal chart of politician Hillary Clinton, Mars at 14 Leo forms a partile square to Karma in Scorpio.

Golf champion Tiger Woods has Jupiter at 15 Aries in direct opposition to Karma.

KASSANDRA 114 [CASSANDRA]

Discovery: July 23, 1871 by Christian Peters.

Backstory: Kassandra was a very skilled seer and prophetess, but often her wearnings were not heeded. Time and again she would make a prediction with accuracy but it would not be heeded, and sometimes disaster ensued. Her frustration gave way to despondency and she eventually took her own life.

Possible Interpretation: Shows where we feel we are not listened to or heard, where we need to bolster our own confidence in our abilities. May also indicate psychic or intuitive skills.

Example: Princess Grace of Monaco, once known as the actress Grace Kelly, had her 19 Scorpio Sun partile opposite Kassandra in Taurus.

KHUFU 3362

Discovery: August 30, 1984 by R. Dunbar.

Backstory: Named for Egyptian pharaoh Khufu, also known as Cheops in Greek, who lived during the 29th century B.C. and was known for building.

B D SALERNO

Possible Interpretation: Bringing creative inspiration into reality; a sense of exploration and discovery.

Example: Famous producer of animated movies and founder of the Disney empire, Walt Disney, had 25 Virgo rising in partile trine to Khufu at 25 Capricorn.

KLIO 84

Discovery: August 25, 1865 by Robert Luther.

Backstory: Associated with history, ancestry, and things of the past.

Possible Interpretation: Shows where the person dwells in the past or has an interest in history; a good storyteller.

Example: In the natal chart of novelist Stephen King, the 27 Virgo Sun conjoins Klio at 28 Virgo.

KLOTHO 97

Discovery: February 17, 1868 by Ernst Tempel.

Backstory: One of the Three Fates of Moirai: first is Klotho, the weaver/beginner of the thread of life that she spins on her wheel. Klotho is associated with the beginning of life. The second is Lachesis – "the Measurer/Apportioner" and the final, somber one is Atropos – "the Unbending/Inflexible One," who cuts the final thread, ending life. Each Fate has her own asteroid which literally reprises her role in mythology. See LACHESIS 120 and ATROPOS 273.

Possible Interpretation: Indicates the beginning of things and where stories of people and events get started; how we spin or perceive experiences in order to adapt to circumstances. I have seen it in crime charts where a web, or narrative, was spun to present a situation in a certain light, and not always an accurate narrative, depending on the asteroid's placement.

Examples: Klotho at 20 Capricorn conjoins the 21 Capricorn Mercury of serial child molester Jeffrey Epstein, who spun a narrative about helping underage girls by providing them with jobs and money.

In the natal chart of actor Christopher Reeve, his 12 Sagittarius Moon was exactly conjunct Klotho. He suffered an extremely difficult fate, becoming a quadriplegic after a fall from a horse.

Handbag designer Kate Spade had her Moon at 6 Sagittarius in trine to Klotho at 5 Aries. In her case I believe the asteroid related to her creation of handbags, which required the handling of materials which are measured, cut, and fashioned to create a design.

KLYTIA 73

Discovery: April 7, 1862 by Horace Tuttle.

Backstory: She was a Greek oceanid, daughter of Titans. Klytia pined away for Apollo, but he had another lover and spurned her. She ran to Apollo's future father-in-law, who took it upon himself to kill his own daughter to punish Apollo. Hopeful of getting together with him, though, she was once again rejected by him, and spent the rest of her life seated on a rock pining away until she died.

Possible Interpretation: Shows where we feel jealousy and insecurity; where lack of self-worth leads to gossip, misdeeds and extreme behaviors, usually related to unrequited love.

Example: Eleanor Roosevelt, wife of President Franklin Roosevelt, had Mars at 19 Scorpio conjoined to Klytia; both she and her husband had clandestine relationships.

LACHESIS 120

B D SALERNO

Discovery: April 10, 1872 by Alphonse Borrelly.

Backstory: The Measurer of the cycles of life, second of the Three Fates of Moirai. Her job was to measure out a thread representing the length of life, and when it was deemed time for that life to be over, her sister Atropos cut the thread.

Possible Interpretation: Show where one measures, plans things carefully, keeps good track of things and firms up boundaries (unless poorly aspected, when the opposite may be true).

Examples: Cesar Chavez, an activist who defended the rights of immigrant workers and various strikes during the 1960s, had Lachesis at 0 Libra in exact trine to his 0 Gemini Midheaven. He helped to define what conditions should be acceptable for migrant workers.

Supermodel Gisele Bundchen has Venus at 19 Gemini partile conjunct Lachesis. It is interesting to consider that all her garments need to be perfectly fitted and measured before each photo shoot.

In the natal chart of television celebrity and lifestyle expert Martha Stewart, Mars at 16 Aries partile squares Lachesis in Cancer. Home design, cooking, and arranging social events all call for measurements—of time, budget, ingredients, and space.

LACRIMOSA 208

Discovery: October 21, 1879 by Johann Palisa.

Backstory: Named for Virgin Mary, Our Lady of Sorrows, means "tearful" in Italian. "Lacrima" means "tear" in Latin.

Possible Interpretation: This asteroid represents where we experience loss or feel grief.

Example: In the natal chart of Eugenie, Princess of York, Mars at 22 Aquarius partile trines Lacrimosa in Libra.

LAETITIA 39

Discovery: February 8, 1856 by Jean Chacomac.

Backstory: Roman goddess of gaiety.

Possible Interpretation: Where the individual experiences joy and pleasure.

Example: In the natal chart of supermodel Cindy Crawford, the 22 Cancer Ascendant is exactly conjoined to Laetitia.

LAMEIA 248

Discovery: June 5, 1885 by Johann Palisa.

Backstory: Lameia, a consort of Zeus, bore him several children, but wife Hera killed them all out of a raging jealousy. Lameia was driven to such intense grief and emotional stress that she then took to killing young men and children.

Possible Interpretation: May show a mentally unbalanced spouse, severe grief over loss of a child, a traumatic family episode, or some association or exposure to crimes involving children.

Example: In the natal chart of Anne Morrow Lindbergh, discussed above under HAUMEA 136108, the asteroid Lameia sits exactly in the position of Algol, at 26 Taurus. Although she went on to have more children, she grieved the loss of little Charlie, her firstborn, for the rest of her life.

LEDA 37

Discovery: January 12, 1856 by Jean Chacoman.

B D SALERNO

Backstory: Mother of the beautiful Helen of Troy and Greek queen of Sparta. She was seduced by Zeus and, in addition to Helen, bore him Castor, Polydeuces, and Clytemnestra, although at the time she was married to Tyndareus.

Possible Interpretation: As the mother of a beautiful, desirable celebrity, and one who got around quite well on her own account, I believe Leda may signify one whose mother was attractive in some way; possible similarities between mother and daughter in terms of socializing, relationships, and notoriety.

LELEĀKŪHONUA 541132

Discovery: October 13, 2005 at Mauna Kea Observatory. TNO.

Backstory: The name was chosen by students in the Hawaiian-language program A Hua He Inoa. The orbit of the massive asteroid, which is beyond the orbit of Neptune, called to mind the migrations of the kolea, or Pacific golden plover bird, which migrates from Alaska to Hawaii.

The Hawaiian yields lele ("fly") + ā ("until") + kū ("stand, appear") + honua ("earth, land").

Possible Interpretation: Suggests a desire to return to one's origin, whether it be one's physical home location, one's ancestral roots, or in a spiritual sense, a return and connection to Source. It may signify one's exploration and travel through consciousness in order to return "home" fulfilled.

Examples: In the natal chart of David Rockefeller, of the dynasty by the same name, Venus at 26 Taurus (which conjoins Algol!) squares this asteroid at 25 Aquarius; wealth and powerful bloodlines helped carve out his destiny.

ASTEROIDS OUR COSMIC INFLUENCERS

Michael Aquino, Lieutenant Colonel of Psychological Operations, US Army, and founder of the Temple of Set, had Jupiter at 4 Scorpio exactly in trine to Leleākūhonua in Pisces.

LEMPO 47171

Discovery: October 1, 1999 by American astronomers Eric Rubenstein and Louis-Gregory Strolger. TNO.

Backstory: A character in Finnish mythology who is a deity of love, fertility, and sexuality. Somewhere along the way, however, he began to do evil deeds, and is also considered a god of evil. He acted primarily out of his own passions with little regard for others.

Possible Interpretation: May signify a person who comes across initially as likable, but who turns another face over time; someone whose self-interest comes first; a seducer, a charismatic narcissist.

Examples: Actress Natalie Wood had Saturn at 17 Aries in her seventh house, representing her partner, in exact trine to Lempo in Sagittarius; her death by drowning while out on her yacht with her husband has long been considered suspicious.

J. Edgar Hoover, head of the FBI for many decades, had Saturn at 5 Scorpio in partile opposition to Lempo.

Allen Dulles, longest serving CIA director (1953-1961) and a bitter enemy of President John F. Kennedy, had Sun at 3 Taurus opposing Lempo at 2 Scorpio, which also trined his 3 Pisces Ascendant.

LETO 68

Discovery: April 29, 1861 by Robert Luther.

Backstory: Mother of Apollo and Artemis (Diana), Leto was a minor goddess of motherhood and fertility.

B D SALERNO

Possible Interpretation: She may represent these traits in the nativity: maternal qualities, a desire or love for children or creativity. If badly aspected, may indicate the opposite.

Example: In the natal chart of Kris Jenner, mother of the Kardashian clan, her 28 Scorpio Ascendant trines Leto at 28 Pisces.

In the natal chart of former President Jimmy Carter, Leto at 22 Leo exactly conjoins the North Node.

LEUKOTHEA 35

Discovery: April 19, 1855 by Robert Luther.

Backstory: Greek goddess of harmony, who later became Ino, a sea goddess who helped Odysseus on his journeys.

Possible Interpretation: References someone who is helpful; possible connection to bodies of water or swimming.

Example: Supermodel Cindy Crawford has her 13 Pisces Moon exactly conjunct Leukothea. She was a swimsuit model in the prime of her career.

LIBERATRIX 125

Discovery: September 11, 1872 by Prosper Henry.

Backstory: This asteroid was dually named for French President Charles deGaulle and also, Jeanne d'Arc (Joan of Arc).

Possible Interpretation: A strong leader for the cause of his/her country, an interest in politics or government, a freedom fighter.

LIE 26955

Discovery: June 30, 1997 by Paul G. Comba.

ASTEROIDS OUR COSMIC INFLUENCERS

Backstory: Named for Norwegian mathematician Marius Sophus Lie.

Possible Interpretation: It is as it sounds. When strongly placed in a chart, can show deception, especially pertaining to a personal or business relationship or deal; also where one is susceptible to manipulation, deceit, or self-deception; where we get drawn into fantasy or illusion.

Example: Junk bond guru Michael Milken, who charmed Wall Street into the frenzy of junk bond investing, with harsh consequences, had Lie at 25 Taurus conjunct the fixed star Caput Algol.

LILITH 1181

Discovery: February 11, 1927 by Benjamin Jekhowsky.

Backstory: In Jewish mythology Lilith was an angel who adored Lucifer but abandoned him after his fall from grace. Lilith was the first human woman created by God from dust and placed in the Garden of Eden with Adam, but problems arose because she refused to be dominated by him. She stole Adam's seed while he slept and gave birth to demons. Determined to dominate Adam, she attempted to have sex with him before the creation of the more submissive Eve.

Possible Interpretation: Lilith may show what we harbor in our own shadow; our dark side that needs exploration and understanding before we can experience true spiritual growth. May show the destructive side of feminine power and abuse of it; it typically indicates the negative expression of the shadow.

Examples: In the natal chart of Anton LaVey, founder of the Church of Satan, Lilith at 6 Aquarius partile squares Venus at 6 Taurus.

In the natal chart of British serial killer Rosemary "Rose" West, Lilith at 22 Libra partile squares Uranus at 22 Cancer.

In the natal chart of politician Hillary Clinton, her 28 Pisces Moon conjoins Lilith at 29 Pisces.

Celebrity Oprah Winfrey has Sun at 8 Aquarius in square to Lilith at 8 Scorpio.

LIRIOPE 414

Discovery: January 16, 1896 by Auguste Charlois.

Backstory: A woodland nymph and mother of Narcissus, famous Greek narcissist. She consulted a seer to determine if her beautiful son would have a long life, to which the seer replied yes, but only if he does not come to know himself. The rest is history – young Narcissus, renowned for his handsomeness, fell in love with his image reflected in a pond, and when he reached for himself he fell into the pond and drowned – he came to know himself - prophecy fulfilled.

Her name means "Face of the Narcissus" from the Greek words "leirion" (narcissus) and "ops" (face). Liriope is also the name for a perennial evergreen plant.

Possible Interpretation: May reference an extremely attractive person who experiences narcissism in some form within the family, relationships, or social arena; difficulty with children.

Example: President Joe Biden has his Moon at 13 Leo in exact opposition to Liriope.

LITVA 2577

Discovery: March 12, 1975 by Nikolai Chernykh.

Backstory: Named for the former USSR Lithuanian state of Russia.

Possible Interpretation: May relate to this country or the former USSR, or something transformed from its former meaning, as was the country after the dissolution of the Union of Soviet Socialist Republics.

Example: Russian President Vladimir Putin has Mercury at 23 Libra trine Attila at 24 Aquarius, and in square to Litva at 24 Capricorn.

LOGOS 58534

Discovery: February 4, 1997 by Mauna Kea Observatory. TNO.

Backstory: From the Greek word meaning knowledge.

Possible Interpretation: Represents integrity and commitment to one's own beliefs; intelligent and rational thought; searching for truth and wisdom.

Examples: Queen Christina of the Netherlands has Mars at 18 Aquarius in exact trine to Logos in Gemini.

In the natal chart of Hindu spiritualist Paramahansa Yogananda, Mars at 5 Aries conjoins Logos at 6 Aries.

LUCIFER 1930

Discovery: October 29, 1964 by Elizabeth Roemer.

Backstory: The asteroid was named after Lucifer, the "shining one" or "light-bearer" from the Hebrew Bible. The light illuminates the dark side of humanity, encouraging us to connect with our shadow, without which we can't achieve true enlightenment.

Possible Interpretation: Shows where the unbridled ego supersedes all other considerations; where one is deceptive, manipulative, dishonest; where one responds to primal unfiltered instincts.

The interpretation need not always be automatically negative; Lucifer shows where the person's shadow faults lie, where egotism, negativity and selfishness may overshadow the personality and pose problems in life.

Examples: Chicago mobster Al Capone had his 14 Aries Moon partile trine Lucifer in Leo.

Noted diplomat, race car driver, and notorious playboy Porfirio Rubirosa had his South Node at 25 Sagittarius conjunct Lucifer and trine Dionysus at 25 Leo.

President-elect Donald Trump has Jupiter at 17 Libra in partile square to Lucifer in Cancer.

LUCINA 146

Discovery: June 8, 1875 by Alphonse Borrelly.

Backstory: Her name means "little light" in Italian; she was a Roman goddess of childbirth, bringing babies into the light.

Possible Interpretation: References childbirth, motherhood, fertility; one who brightens things.

Example: Child beauty pageant queen JonBenet Ramsay had her 13 Leo Sun exactly conjunct Lucina; even at the age of six she was known for her sparkling personality.

LUST 4386

Discovery: September 24, 1988 by Antonin Mrkos and Milos Tichy.

Backstory: The name conveys its meaning, which is not always lust of a sexual nature, but a deeper, more intense desire and drive for something.

Possible Interpretation: Represents what arouses us, our sexual expression, the pursuit of pleasure and our deepest desires, which are not always sexual. Can also indicate the object of physical lust and desire; what we lust after.

Examples: Ukrainian President Volodymyr Zelenskyy has his 17 Leo Moon trine Thalia at 18 Sagittarius; prior to joining politics he was an actor and performed as a clown, which prepared him well for his next gig. Moon, Thalia, and Lust at 18 Aries form a grand trine.

LUTETIA 20

Discovery: November 15, 1852 by Hermann Goldschmidt.

Backstory: Lutetia in Latin means "marsh" or "swamp," and was the name of an ancient settlement of the Gallic tribe on the south bank of the River Seine in Paris.

Possible Interpretation: There is little on its significance, but I venture a guess that it may show some connection to France, French culture, or subjects of historical interest in an individual's chart. It may also simply refer to swampy or marshy areas, which may prove useful in a forensic horoscope.

LYSISTRATA 897

Discovery: August 3, 1918 by Max Wolf.

Backstory: She was the heroine of a Greek comedy. Lysistrata engineered an all-female protest, withholding sex from the men of Greece until they stopped going to war.

Possible Interpretation: May show sexual or other charms that are used for manipulative purposes or to achieve a specific goal; social activism.

B D SALERNO

MAJA 66

Discovery: April 9, 1861 by Horace Tuttle.

Backstory: One of the Seven Sisters of the Pleiades, daughter of Atlas and mother of Hermes (Mercury). She represents the month of May, springtime, fertility and the blossoming of new growth, be it physical or metaphysical.

Possible Interpretation: May show where the individual is creative, where they can regenerate and heal themselves, where they can start anew.

MAKEMAKE 136472

Discovery: March 31, 2005 by a team led by Michael E. Brown. Dwarf Planet.

Backstory: Makemake is Rapa Nui language for the god of creation and fertility of the Polynesian inhabitants of Easter Island in the South Pacific.

Possible Interpretation: Shows our connection to our natural surroundings, the earth; creating a harmonious environment; fertility; creativity.

Examples: Popular sitcom actor Matthew Perry had Eris at 12 Aries in partile trine to Mars in Sagittarius, with the grand trine filled out by Makemake at 12 Leo.

In the natal chart of celebrity Kris Jenner, mother to the Kardashian clan, Venus at 29 Scorpio trines Makemake at 28 Cancer.

In the natal chart of Queen Beatrix of the Netherlands, her 6 Capricorn Midheaven is exactly opposed by Makemake; she has expressed concerns over problems facing the environment and the future of the planet.

MANIAC 228029

Discovery: April 2, 2008 by Juan LaCruz.

Backstory: Not found. I wonder if the name relates to an eccentric orbit or behavior of the asteroid, as some of them are definitely erratic.

Possible Interpretation: It is as it sounds: mentally unstable, psychological challenges, extreme nervous stress. However, lest we be too quick to apply a label of mental health problems, it's also worth considering that this may indicate a person who just thinks and/or acts outside the box, is uniquely original and unconventional, and for those flimsy reasons may be unfairly judged by conventional society. In general, though, I have found this asteroid in significant placement in the charts of killers and psychopaths, as shown below.

Examples: In the natal chart of French serial strangler Henri Landru, Venus at 29 Capricorn is partile conjunct Maniac, which also conjoins the South Node.

British serial killer Fred West has Mars at 20 Aries trine Maniac at 19 Leo, which is partile conjunct Sedna.

George Lincoln Rockwell, founder of the American Nazi Party, had Maniac at 26 Gemini partile square his 26 Virgo Moon and next to his 27 Gemini North Node.

In the natal chart of occultist and rocket scientist Jack Parsons, Mercury at 23 Pisces conjoins Maniac at 22 Pisces.

Casey Anthony, who was acquitted of the murder of her baby daughter Caylee Marie, has Maniac at 18 Gemini in square to her 19 Pisces

Ascendant; she was extremely deceptive in her statements to the police, and was caught in numerous lies about the crime.

In the natal chart of Marshall Applewhite, founder of the suicidal religious group Heaven's Gate, his 22 Taurus Moon opposed Maniac at 23 Scorpio. In 1997 his 39 followers all drank poison so that their souls could be reunited in space travel with the Hale-Bopp comet.

Israeli Prime Minister Benjamin Netanyahu has Venus at 12 Sagittarius in trine to Medea at 13 Aries; Venus is also in square to Maniac at 12 Virgo.

MANWE 385446

Discovery: August 25, 2003 by Marc Buie. TNO.

Backstory: Manwe was a character in the writings of J.R.R. Tolkien, who brought us the *Lord of the Rings* trilogy. In *Silmarillion* Manwe was chief of fourteen archangels who created the world.

Possible Interpretation: References resurrection through coming to terms with our karmic debts; rebirth; where we are transformed by fateful circumstances.

Examples: Women's tennis champion Martina Navratilova has her 14 Virgo Venus partile conjunct Manwe. She has overcome major challenges in her recent bouts with throat and breast cancer.

J. Robert Oppenheimer, called "the father of the atomic bomb," had Mercury at 21 Taurus opposite Manwe at 22 Scorpio.

In the natal chart of Pope Francis, his 25 Sagittarius Sun is partile conjunct Manwe.

MASSALIA 19

ASTEROIDS OUR COSMIC INFLUENCERS

Discovery: September 19, 1852 by Annibale de Gasparis.

Backstory: It is the Latin name for the southern coastal French city of Marseille. It is also the main body of a large belt of asteroids thought to be the fragments of a collision with Massalia.

Possible Interpretation: May indicate some connection to that part of the country, France, or the French culture; loyalty to family or strong interest in the protection of a bloodline or a community.

MBABAMWANAWARESA 341520

Discovery: March 11, 2005 by Marc Buie. TNO.

Backstory: Named after Mbaba Mwana Waresa, a Zulu fertility goddess of Earth and Water.

Possible Interpretation: Represents the spirit of creativity, fertility in terms of where we are most productive, literally or figuratively; where we can be reborn and resurrected.

Examples: The 25 Aquarius Moon of Princess Diana was partile opposite Mbabamwanawaresa in her natal chart.

Pop star Madonna's 23 Leo Sun exactly conjoins this asteroid.

In the natal chart of African-American activist, writer, and educator Booker T. Washington, his 14 Taurus Sun conjoins Mbabamwanawaresa at 15.

MEDEA 212

Discovery: February 6, 1880 by Johann Palisa.

Backstory: Greek sorceress who was married to Jason (of Jason and the Argonauts). Jason had sworn to love her forever, but when she tricked the daughters of King Pelias into killing their own father he left her to marry another. Hell-bent on vengeance she sent a magic robe to his new bride, which erupted into flames, killing her and burning down her palace. Medea then disappeared into a dark cloud carried by two dragons.

Possible Interpretation: May indicate a murderous person in a crime chart, or the tragic loss of children; working with witchcraft and the occult; someone overtaken by their dark side or obsessed with revenge.

Examples: In the natal chart of drug trafficker Pablo Escobar, who was responsible for the deaths of hundreds of people, his Sun at 9 Sagittarius partile trines Medea in Aries.

Israeli Prime Minister Benjamin Netanyahu has Venus at 12 Sagittarius in trine to Medea at 13 Aries; Venus is also in square to Maniac at 12 Virgo.

Diplomat, race car driver, and notorious playboy Porfirio Rubirosa had his Mars at 8 Sagittarius conjunct Bacchus at 7; also, Mars was partile conjunct Medea.

MEDUSA 149

Discovery: September 21, 1875 by Henri Joseph Perrotin.

Backstory: Also known as the Gorgon's Head, she was a particularly hideous she-monster with snakes curling out of her head in place of hair. Anyone who gazed upon her was doomed to turn instantly to stone. She was finally decapitated by Perseus, a Greek hero.

Possible Interpretation: References a fearful personage, a monstrous bully, someone who intimidates others through word, appearance, or gesture; can also reference our own dark side, what we find ugly within ourselves; genetically bad hair.

ASTEROIDS OUR COSMIC INFLUENCERS

Examples: Ian Brady, who with his paramour Myra Hindley committed the vicious Moors Murders of children in the Sixties, had his Mercury-Venus superconjunction at 3 Capricorn in partile square to Medusa at 3 Libra. Together the couple formed a dangerous pair of psychopaths who egged each other on to extremes of cruelty and violence. Their names appear again in the examples.

Another British serial murdering couple was Fred West and his wife Rosemary. His 24 Capricorn Moon squared Medusa at 24 Libra.

British serial killer Dennis Nilsen, a gay man who murdered his male sex partners, had the Moon at 18 Cancer partile opposite Medusa.

MELANCHOLIA 5708

Discovery: October 12, 1977 by Paul Wild.

Backstory: The word originates with the Greek melan, meaning "black," and cholē, meaning "bile." Doctors in earlier times believed in a system of humors or bodily fluids that affected behavior. These included black or dark bile, yellow bile, blood, and phlegm. Any imbalance in these substances led to physical or mental illness.

Possible Interpretation: As the name suggests, melancholy or depression; a deep longing akin to nostalgia for times or things gone; a tinge of sadness; where we experience such feelings and what they are about is shown in the horoscope.

Example: Actor/producer/director Clint Eastwood's Ascendant at 18 Scorpio trines Melacholia exactly in Cancer; many of his movies convey a sense of gravitas, portraying characters whose good days are behind them.

MELETE 56

Discovery: September 9, 1857 by Hermann Goldschmidt.

B D SALERNO

Backstory: She is the Muse of Meditation in Greek mythology but has also been associated with mental health issues.

Possible Interpretation: May indicate anxiety disorders, panic attacks and other forms of emotional stress.

Examples: Nurse Clara Barton, founder of the American Red Cross, suffered from nervous disorders, depression, and suicidal ideation; Melete at 25 Leo was conjunct her South Node at 26 Leo.

Infamous criminal Charles Manson had Venus at 18 Scorpio in partile square to Melete in Leo.

MELITTA 676

Discovery: January 16, 1909 by P. Melotte.

Backstory: Melitta is the Greek for the name Melissa, a nymph of ancient Greek mythology, and possibly also a nod to its discoverer, Melotte. Melissa means "honeybee."

Possible Interpretation: I venture a guess that there is some association with bees, therefore, pollination, fertility, childbirth.

Example: In the natal chart of former President Jimmy Carter, Venus at 23 Leo partile conjoins Melitta; he was a very successful peanut farmer before becoming President.

MELPOMENE 18

Discovery: June 24, 1852 by John Russell Hind.

Backstory: One of the nine Muses, daughters of Zeus and Mnemosyne, she was the Greek Muse of Tragedy.

Possible Interpretation: Her presence in a chart may indicate where we experience painful or tragic losses and emotionally devastating events.

MELUSINA 373

Discovery: September 15, 1893 by Auguste Charlois.

Backstory: Also known by her French name Melusine, she was a mermaid and also a fairy.

Possible Interpretation: May reference someone by the same or similar name; a charming but elusive quality; a mysterious quality; someone who probes the depths of a situation to see it for what it is.

Examples: In the natal chart of President Joe Biden, the Sun at 27 Scorpio partile opposes Melusina.

Eugenie, Princess of York, has Mars at 9 Aquarius partile trine Melusina in Libra.

MEMORIA 1247

Discovery: August 30, 1932 by Marguerite Laugier.

Backstory: Memoria is the Latin word for memory or remembrance, and astronomer Laugier intended its name as a marker for pleasant memories of her time at the Uccle Observatory in 1932.

Possible Interpretation: May show good powers of memory, a knack for remembering detail; drawing upon memories for inspiration; if poorly aspected, may show where memories are unhappy, even traumatic.

Examples: Rock star Courtney Love, whose musician husband Kurt Cobain died during their marriage, has Venus at 20 Gemini trine Memoria at 21 Libra.

In the natal chart of singer Whitney Houston, who passed away at the age of 43 due to accidental drowning, Memoria at 7 Virgo exactly opposes her 8 Pisces Ascendant.

MENTALL 7116

Discovery: December 2, 1986 by Edward Bowell.

Backstory: Named after E. Talmadge "Tal" Mentall, contemporary American astronomy atlas illustrator and draftsman.

Possible Interpretation: Alternate meanings, as we see with so many of the named asteroids. With due respect to Mr. Mentall, the asteroid may indicate a skilled draftsman, one with talent in illustration, or, mental instability, mental health issues, possible derangement.

Examples: In the natal chart of notorious drug trafficker Pablo Escobar, who was known to have psychotic episodes, Mercury at 14 Sagittarius conjoins Mentall at 15, as well as Toro at 15.

In the natal chart of Mafia boss John Gotti, Jupiter, Saturn, and Mentall all join up at 11 Taurus.

MESSALINA 545

Discovery: October 3, 1904 by Paul Götz.

Backstory: Named after Valeria Messalina, the third wife of Roman Emperor Claudius. She was a manipulative, selfish, cruel, and lustful character. She garnished quite a reputation by having a sex marathon to see who could bed the most partners in 24 hours, and she won, having had 25 partners.

ASTEROIDS OUR COSMIC INFLUENCERS

Possible Interpretation: Represents a heavily sexual appetite, skill in manipulating others; someone whose raw desires trump over all other priorities and considerations.

Example: In the natal chart of Yoko Ono, Japanese artist and wife of musician John Lennon, the Moon at 11 Sagittarius partile trines Messalina in Aries.

METIS 9

Discovery: April 25, 1848 by Andrew Graham.

Backstory: Greek oceanid, daughter of Titans Oceanus and Tethys, and mother of Athena. She is the goddess of wisdom. In some versions of Greek mythology, Zeus, fearing that their child might have more powers than he, swallowed Metis. But then Hephaestus chopped open Zeus's head, from whence emerged the brilliant warrior goddess Athena.

Possible Interpretation: She represents wisdom and knowledge, but because of her unfortunate demise, may also indicate someone with a controlling, envious spouse.

MINERVA 93

Discovery: August 24, 1867 by James Craig Watson.

Backstory: The Roman goddess of war whose Greek counterpart was Athena. Known for prowess at war games and strategizing; also, a goddess of beauty, feminine charm, and seduction.

Possible Interpretation: An individual with strong strategic abilities; competitiveness or athleticism; qualities of attractiveness, charisma, charm.

Example: In the natal chart of actress Jennifer Aniston,[****]

B D SALERNO

Robert F. Kennedy Jr. Has his 2 Leo Ascendant partile opposite Minerva.

MIRIAM 102

Discovery: August 22, 1868 by Christian Peters.

Backstory: A Biblical prophetess.

Possible Interpretation: May indicate special intuitive powers, psychic abilities, or someone drawn to psychic phenomena and the supernatural.

Example: Medical intuitive/author/lecturer Caroline Myss has her Moon at 23 Gemini partile square Miriam in Virgo.

MNEMOSYNE 57

Discovery: September 22, 1859 by Robert Luther

Backstory: First generation Titan and lover of Zeus, by whom she bore the nine Muses. Also the Greek goddess of memory.

Possible Interpretation: References memory, and if afflicted natally or by transit, possible memory problems; also, divine inspiration. Shows the people, places or things from which we receive divine inspiration.

Examples: In the natal chart of supermodel Cindy Crawford, the 22 Cancer Ascendant exactly trines both Mnemosyne and Juno at 22 Pisces.

Former President Jimmy Carter had Moon at 13 Scorpio partile conjunct Mnemosyne.

MODESTIA 370

Discovery: July 14, 1893 by Auguste Charlois.

Backstory: The word means "modesty" in Italian; also the name of a Roman goddess.

Possible Interpretation: Meaning "modesty," may show where the person shows restraint, inhibitions or shyness, or if afflicted, where they lack any sense of it.

Example: In the natal chart of actress Ali MacGraw, once married to actor Steve McQueen, her 19 Taurus Ascendant trines Modestia at 18 Capricorn.

MOIRA 638

Discovery: May 5, 1907 by Joel Hastings Metcalf.

Backstory: Moira is derived from the Greek word for Fate; the Three Fates were also called the "Moirai". She is the daughter of Zeus and Themis according to some sources.

Possible Interpretation: Shows the part of life that feels heavily governed by karma; a sense that we cannot escape certain circumstances or situations that seemed destined to occur no matter what.

MORS-SOMNUS 341520

Discovery: October 14, 2007 Chad Trujillo and Scott S. Sheppard. TNO.

Backstory: The name of this Trans-Neptunian body is revealing: "mors" means death in Latin, and "somnus" is sleep. In Roman mythology, Somnus is sleep personified. His Greek counterpart is Hypnos, from which we derive the word hypnosis. Thus the asteroid refers to deep states of consciousness, which is appropriate as this asteroid is located beyond the realm of Neptune, ruling sleep, dreams, the subconscious, and altered states of consciousness.

Possible Interpretation: May indicate the desire to explore and experience various states of altered consciousness, either through meditation, study, drugs, hypnosis, bilocation, or other means. An interest in probing deep spiritual themes, one's own mortality, dream states, universal consciousness, death.

Examples: In the natal chart of rock star Courtney Love, Kurt Cobain's wife at the time of his death, which was considered suspicious, her 23 Cancer Moon opposes Mors-Somnus at 24 Capricorn.

Charles Taze Russell, founder of the Jehovah's Witness religious sect, had Venus at 0 Aries partile conjunct Mors-Somnus. His religion taught that great rewards would come only to the believers of the sect after a massive migration to a new utopian reality.

In the natal chart of singer Whitney Houston, who passed away at the age of 43 due to accidental drowning possibly due to drug intoxication, Mors-Somnus at 21 Capricorn conjuncts her South Node.

Bobbi Kristina Brown, daughter of Whitney Houston, who passed away in the same manner as her mother, also had a strong Mors-Somnus connection: Sun at 14 Pisces partile conjunct Mors-Somnus.

MOSHUP 66391

Discovery: May 20, 1999 by LINEAR Group.

Backstory: Moshup is a heroic giant of the Wampanoag tribe of New England and other coastal tribes of the region who inhabited the region prior to the arrival of Europeans. He sought to establish peaceful coexistence between the people and helped define the areas of Massachusetts now known as Martha's Vineyard and other areas of Cape Cod.

Possible Interpretation: May indicate what must be done in order to obtain one's desired goals; manifestation of one's dreams and objectives.

Example: In the natal chart of Queen Beatrix of the Netherlands, her 6 Capricorn Midheaven is exactly conjoined by Moshup.

MYRRHA 381

Discovery: January 10, 1894 by Auguste Charlois.

Backstory: Myrrha is a young Greek woman who falls in love with her father Cinyras and seduces him into an incestuous relationship by trickery. She gives birth to handsome and physically perfect Adonis [see ADONIS 2101] When he discovers her deception he chases her across Arabia with the intent of killing her. After several months on the run she finally turns to the gods for help. They show mercy to her and, rather than allow her to be killed, they turn her into a myrrh tree.

Possible Interpretation: Represents sexual abuse, molestation, or unconventional sexual relationships such as incest; someone who uses guile to seduce another; resorting to manipulation and trickery to get one's way.

Example: British serial rapist and pedophile Jimmy Savile had Jupiter at 17 Aquarius square Myrrha at 17 Taurus. He had a morbid relationship with his mother, whom he considered the love of his life, and kept her body after her death, dressing it up in various outfits.

NARCISSUS 37117

Discovery: November 1, 2000 by William Kwong Yu Yeung.

Backstory: Narcissus was a handsome Greek man, son of the nymph Liriope, who became enamored of his reflection in a pond. He fell so hard for himself that while staring at himself he literally fell into the pond and drowned. In a birth chart may indicate in what areas one tends to be obsessively fixated and gives little or nothing to others.

Narcissus #37117 has been recently categorized as an "unusual object," according to the Minor Planet Center website (www.minorplanetcenter.org).

Possible Interpretation: Depending on aspects and placements, may show tendency to attract narcissistic personalities – or to be one. The pathology is well studied and was appropriately named "narcissism" or "the Narcissus complex."

Examples: In the natal chart of Dr. Anthony Fauci, Narcissus at 4 Capricorn conjoins his 3 Capricorn Sun.

In the natal chart of serial rapist/killer Ted Bundy, Narcissus at 11 Gemini conjoins the North Node at 12 Gemini.

Hollywood producer and convicted rapist Harvey Weinstein has his Mars at 18 Scorpio conjunct Narcissus at 27.

NAUSIKAA 192

Discovery: February 17, 1879 by Johann Palisa.

Backstory: Greek princess in Homer's epic poem *Odyssey,* about the adventures and travels of its hero Odysseus. She provided aid to Odysseus.

Possible Interpretation: No information was available. I venture a guess that it references helpfulness and support, as Nausikaa helped Odysseus during his travels and tribulations.

NEFERTITI 3199

Discovery: September 13, 1982 by Eugene and Carolyn Shoemaker.

ASTEROIDS OUR COSMIC INFLUENCERS

Backstory: Named for the ancient Egyptian queen Nefertiti (ca. 1370–1330 BC), mother-in-law of pharaoh Tutankhamun and Chief King's Wife of Akhenaten of the 18th dynasty. She was known for promoting the worship of the god Aten. [see ATEN 2062]

Possible Interpretation: May denote beauty, elegance and grace; awareness and connection with one's own inner power; observance of divine intelligence.

Example: Lifestyle expert and television celebrity Martha Stewart has Mercury at 25 Cancer exactly conjunct Nefertiti.

NEMAUSA 51

Discovery: January 22, 1858 by Joseph Jean Pierre Laurent.

Backstory: Celtic god Nemausus, the patron god of Nimes, France during the Roman era. The asteroid was named "in memory and honor of the city and the fountain of the god Nemausus." At that time the names were feminized, and so Nemausus became Nemausa.

Possible Interpretation: May reference a connection to Celtic lore or France; also, one who seeks retribution in response to wrongdoings.

NEMESIS 128

Discovery: November 25, 1872 by James Craig Watson.

Backstory: Greek goddess of revenge, appropriately designated by the arrow of Mars pointing earthward, exacting revenge. Nemesis was there to ensure that no bad deed went unpunished.

Possible Interpretation: Showing where one is opposed by others, in what area one faces retribution, or their own downfall through another's desire for revenge. Seeking vengeance or being at the other end of it.

Examples: Serial killer Dennis Rader, a.k.a the "B-T-K (Bind, Torture, Kill)" monster, has Nemesis at 23 Pisces partile opposite Jupiter.

In the natal chart of pop star Taylor Swift, her Moon at 5 Cancer is directly opposite Nemesis; she has had open feuds with other celebrities, and has also had issues with stalkers.

JonBenet Ramsey's natal chart shows Venus at 20 Cancer in partile trine to Nemesis at 20 Pisces.

In the natal chart of Branch Davidian religious extremist David Koresh, the Midheaven at 1 Cancer is partile conjunct Nemesis, which also opposes Saturn at 2 Capricorn.

In the natal chart of former President Richard M. Nixon, the 20 Aquarius Moon is exactly conjunct Nemesis; he was forced to resign over fallout from the Watergate scandal, which was engineered by members of his own staff.

NEPHELE 431

Discovery: December 18, 1897 by Auguste Charlois.

Backstory: She is the mother of many centaurs through her relationship with Ixion, and ruled over the clouds.

Possible Interpretation: May reference clouds, fog, smog; where we do not see clearly or seeing beyond the normal.

Example: In the natal chart of Indian spiritual leader and activist Mahatma Gandhi, Venus at 16 Aries partile opposes Nephele.

Mentalist "the Amazing Kreskin" (George Joseph Kresge, Jr.) had Sun at 21 Capricorn conjunct Nephele at 22.

NEPHTHYS 287

ASTEROIDS OUR COSMIC INFLUENCERS

Discovery: August 25, 1889 by Christian Peters.

Backstory: Egyptian goddess, younger sister of Isis, Osiris, and Seth. Legend tells us that she had an affair with Osiris and gave birth to the god Anubis, ruler of the dead and the underworld. She is sometimes depicted as a hawk guarding over the funeral bier of Osiris.

Possible Interpretation: Interest or association with death in some way, or rebirth, or transformation; delving deeply into the inner realms of the spirit and the unconscious.

Example: Actress Natalie Wood, whose early death by drowning in 1981 saddened the world, had Jupiter at 0 Pisces exactly opposite Nephthys in Virgo.

NERTHUS 601

Discovery: June 21, 1906 by Max Wolf.

Backstory: A Danish goddess of fertility and peace, thought to be the female counterpart of the Viking god Njord. She had a cult following, and her statue would be driven around in an ox-drawn cart for all to see and admire, after which the cart had to be thoroughly cleansed and all attendants who had touched or cleaned it had to be slain to preserve its purity.

Possible Interpretation: References fertility and creativity, also strength in terms of winning over others; fertility may be evident not just in large numbers of children but in production and creation of works and contributions to society.

Example: Mahatma Gandhi, famous political and spiritual leader of India who preached non-violent resistance, had a 25 Libra Ascendant in partile trine to Nerthus.

NESSUS 7066

B D SALERNO

Discovery: April 26, 1993 by David Rabinowitz. Centaur.

Backstory: He was a Greek centaur, half man and half beast, and the beast part got the better of him. He offered to carry Dejaneira, wife of Heracles, across a river on his back, but midway through he attempted to rape her. Heracles immediately responded by killing him with a poisoned arrow.

Possible Interpretation: Represents rape, sexual molestation, or sexual abuse in either a natal or crime chart; desire to dominate or control.

Examples: Sadly, Nessus is prominent in the crime chart of young JonBenet Ramsey, as well as other disturbing asteroids like Lust and Dejaneira, representing a person or persons who cruelly stole her life at the age of six.

In the natal chart of SpaceX founder Elon Musk, Venus at 19 Gemini partile conjoins Nessus.

Convicted sex trafficker Ghislaine Maxwell, former partner in crime with Jeffrey Epstein, has Saturn at 28 Capricorn exactly trine Nessus in Taurus.

Prince Andrew of Britain, who was embroiled in a sex scandal connected to Ghislaine Maxwell and associates, has Nessus at 24 Taurus opposite his 25 Scorpio Moon.

In the crime event chart of JonBenet Ramsey, Venus at 11 Sagittarius is exactly conjunct Nessus.

NIKE 307

Discovery: March 5, 1891 by Auguste Charlois.

Backstory: Greek goddess of victory, may also represent Nice, France.

Possible Interpretation: Competitiveness, love of competition; drive for success, to be the best, where one succeeds best.

Example: In the natal chart of basketball champion Michael Jordan, his 9 Leo Mars is exactly conjunct Nike, the athletic shoe brand that has produced his own line of Air Jordan.

NIOBE 71

Discovery: August 13, 1861 by Robert Luther.

Backstory: She was the Greek daughter of Tantalus who angered the gods. They retaliated by killing her seven sons and daughters and turned her into a rock.

Possible Interpretation: Represents extreme grief, sorrow, loss; death of a child.

Examples: In the natal chart of Patsy Ramsey, mother of slain child pageant queen JonBenet Ramsey, Niobe at 8 Capricorn exactly conjoins her Sun.

In the natal chart of theoretical physicist Albert Einstein, Niobe at 24 Cancer widely opposes his Mars at 26 Capricorn. He had an illegitimate daughter, Lieserl, who died of scarlet fever at the age of one.

In the natal chart of kidnap victim Johnny Gosch, Jupiter at 29 Libra exactly conjoins Niobe.

NOFRETETE 1068

Discovery: September 13, 1926 by Eugène Delporte.

Backstory: The asteroid was named after the Ancient Egyptian Queen Nefertiti by its German name "Nofretete". The near-Earth asteroid Nefertiti 3199 is also named after her; see also NEFERTITI 3199.

B D SALERNO

Possible Interpretation: May denote beauty, elegance and grace; awareness and connection with one's own inner power; observance of divine intelligence.

Examples: Dr. Jack Kevorkian, named the "doctor of death" because he performed assisted suicides for terminally ill patients, had Mars at 7 Aries partile square Nofretete at 7 Cancer.

In the natal chart of actress Nicole Kidman, Moon at 13 Sagittarius partile opposes Nofretete.

NOSTALGIA 3162

Discovery: December 16, 1980 by Edward Bowell.

Backstory: What we miss or long for from the past. The word originates from the Greek "nostos" and "algos" - returning home to pain.

Possible Interpretation: What we miss or long for from the past; things that stir memories and emotions, a sense of something missing or gone.

NUWA 150

Discovery: October 18, 1875 by James Craig Watson.

Backstory: Named after the Chinese creator goddess.

Possible Interpretation: References fertility, so may indicate where we are creative or original in our endeavors, or otherwise, a very fertile person, with many children or accomplishments. An originator or creator of new ideas.

Example: In the natal chart of Queen Beatrix of the Netherlands, her 10 Aquarius Sun squares Nuwa at 11 Taurus; she has been outspoken over concerns for the future of the planet and the need for environmental reforms.

NYCTIMENE 2150

Discovery: October 13, 1977 by William Sebok.

Backstory: Nyctimene has a particularly painful history and is regarded as one of the more tragic women in Greek mythology. She was the daughter of a prominent man who desired her and forced her into a sexual relationship. Although the situation was out of her control she was still shunned by her community and blamed for the illicit relationship – it wasn't fun being a woman back then. Shamed and disgraced, she hid herself away in the forest, only coming out at night. She was turned into an owl by Athena, owls being nocturnal birds.

Possible Interpretation: Depending on placement in the birth horoscope, may indicate issues of incest, rape, or abuse by the father or father figure; sexual molestation; misogyny.

NYSA 44

Discovery: May 27, 1857 by Hermann Goldschmidt.

Backstory: Named after a mythical mountain land in Greece where the rain nymphs and the Hyades went to play.

Possible Interpretation: A mental playground where ideas can materialize; the concept or ideal of a special space for the individual to aspire to or dream about.

Examples: In the natal chart of pop star Taylor Swift, Moon at 5 Cancer is directly opposite Nysa.

In the natal chart of Eugenie, Princess of York, NYSA at 15 Aquarius conjoins the North Node in the same degree.

B D SALERNO

ODIN 3989

Discovery: September 8, 1986 by Poul B. Jensen.

Backstory: Odin, or Othin, is a prominent deity in Norse Viking mythology, much like Zeus to the Greeks and Jupiter to the Romans. He rules over warrior spirits and had power over them by influencing their thoughts and actions to direct the course of battle.

He was capable of shape-shifting, abilities akin to that of the shaman, and he communicated with the dead in order to gain more knowledge into occult and magical practices. He was known to wander the earth in disguise, and his symbol is the raven. He was betrothed to Frigga or Freija; see FRIGGA 77 and FREIJA 76.

Possible Interpretation: May indicate a strong, aggressive nature; interest in the occult, magical practices, mind control; intelligence, charisma and leadership qualities.

ODYSSEUS 1143

Discovery: January 28, 1930 by Karl Reinmuth.

Backstory: Odysseus is the hero of the epic poems *Iliad* and *Odyssey* by the Greek writer Homer. He was a Greek prince who traveled to Troy to ask for the hand of the beautiful Helen, who had many suitors.

Upon noticing this he became aware that the stiff competition for her hand could instigate a war – which it did – so he departed upon a journey of many years, facing many dangerous challenges along the way. He was known as a courageous warrior, gifted with cunning and guile, and also very bold and adventurous.

Possible Interpretation: May indicate a strong leader who is not afraid to face new challenges; one with a desire or need to wander or travel;

boldness and cleverness in the areas highlighted by the asteroid. A quick and agile mind, embracing all that a new discovery can bring.

OENONE 215

Discovery: April 7, 1880 by Viktor Knorre.

Backstory: A Greek nymph who was the wife of Paris of Troy; she was known to possess the gift of healing, but when Paris abandoned her for Helen, she became resentful and sought vengeance.

Possible Interpretation: May represent where we experience difficult emotions due to relationship stresses; where we wish to avenge hurts and offenses, where we may stray from ideas of right and wrong in order to do so.

Example: Oenone at 18 Scorpio forms a partile trine with Mercury in Pisces in the nativity of singer/songwriter Lady Gaga.

OHNO 5180

Discovery: April 6, 1989 by Tetsuya Fujii and Kazuo Watanabe.

Backstory: Named for Japanese software engineer Keiko Ohno. Also taken literally by some astrologers to mean "oh, no!"

Possible Interpretation: I venture a guess that it means where we are embarrassed, unprepared, or surprised; where we try to hide something to avoid exposure.

Example: In the natal chart of celebrity Sean Combs, a.k.a "P. Diddy," Mercury at 4 Scorpio partile squares Ohno at 4 Leo; considering his recent scandals he has no doubt had many "oh, no!" moments.

OKYRHOE 52872

Discovery: September 18, 1998 by Skywatch. Centaur.

Backstory: A Greek nymph, the daughter of the centaur Chiron and the water nymph Chariklo [see CHIRON 2060 and CHARIKLO 10199]. The word means fast flowing or running.

Possible Interpretation: Ability to cope with attacks from others and stand up for oneself in the face of criticism; defending oneself from hostilities; an ability to navigate rough waters.

Examples: In the natal chart of politician Kamala Harris, Venus at 17 Virgo squares Okyrhoe at 18 Sagittarius.

Famed nurse Clara Barton, founder of the Red Cross, had 1 Capricorn at her Midheaven partile conjunct Okyrhoe.

Jessica Lynch, a U.S. Marine who was rescued from captivity during Operation Desert Storm, has Okyrhoe at 5 Leo opposite her 6 Aquarius Midheaven.

OPHELIA 171

Discovery: January 13, 1877 by Alphonse Borrelly.

Backstory: A tragic character in Shakepeare's *Hamlet*. Although her name is from the Greek word meaning "help," or "gain," she is not a character in Greek mythology. In Shakespeare's play she is engaged to Hamlet, Prince of Denmark, but is done grievously wrong by him, after which she loses her mind, which leads to her drowning; thus, her existence in classical literature as a tragic figure.

Possible Interpretation: Accidental drowning; insanity and death by drowning, unrequited love, heartbreak; feeling inundated or overwhelmed, female delusion driven to madness; heartbreak; obsession.

Although asteroid Ophelia has many themes, some astrologers have noticed a link between this asteroid and drownings.

Examples: Perhaps the world's most famous pedophile, Jimmy Savile, had Mercury at 0 degree Sagittarius trine Ophelia at 0 Leo. He had a bizarre relationship with his mother, a tragic figure whose body he kept after her death, dressing her up and then changing her clothes. He called her the "love of my life," but his mother was very disturbed over the "terrible darkness" that sometimes overcame him.

In the natal chart of Pope Francis, Mars at 19 Libra partile opposes Ophelia.

In the natal chart of Elvis Presley, Mercury at 22 Capricorn exactly opposes Ophelia. He had an extreme emotional attachment to his mother, whose death was devastating for him.

ORCUS 90482

Discovery: February 17, 2004 by Michael Brown, Chad Trujillo and David Rabinowitz. TNO.

Backstory: Orcus is the Etruscan and Roman god for death and the underworld, who punishes those who have committed wrongdoing. It is sometimes called "anti-Pluto" because the two bodies are directly opposite in their orbit.

Possible Interpretation: Indicates where karma is exacted in the lifetime due to previous harm done to others. In view of its nickname "anti-Pluto," suffering karmic payments with the intent of transforming one's karma certainly fits into this profile.

Examples: Actress Jean Seberg, who took her own life due to constant surveillance by three-letter agencies, had Mercury at 9 Sagittarius partile opposite Orcus, which suggests a heavily karmic involvement with government authorities.

B D SALERNO

In the natal chart of Chicago mobster Al Capone, his 13 Pisces Ascendant conjoins Orcus; he literally had heavy debt to the government, karmic and otherwise.

Joe Valachi, the first mobster to turn federal witness against the Mafia, had his Sun at 29 Virgo exactly opposite Orcus.

ORIUS 330836

Discovery: November 9, 1999 by Takao Kobayashi. Centaur.

Backstory: Orius is a Trans-Neptunian Object whose name means "of the mountain."

Possible Interpretation: Highlights the faith one puts in values and value systems; how we approach material goals; how one manifests their creative drive.

Examples: Former mobster Sammy "the Bull" Gravano has Sun at 21 Pisces conjunct Orius at 20; his value systems were aligned with those of organized crime.

In the natal chart of President-elect Donald Trump, Venus at 25 Cancer exactly trines Orius in Pisces.

ORNAMENTA 350

Discovery: December 14, 1892 by Auguste Charlois.

Backstory: Named for the daughter of a Dutch sailor and member of a French astronomical society. This asteroid belongs to a large family of between 1 and 93 asteroids that share similar spectral properties and orbital elements. This could mean they originated from the same object.

Possible Interpretation: Not much information was found. I included this asteroid only because I noted that it often appeared in charts run on asteroid software. Based on the facts above, however, I will venture a flimsy guess that it relates to one's connection to one's roots, family, ancestry, etc.

I am also tempted to spin the idea of "ornamentation" but will leave that up to the reader's imagination. The example below is revealing.

Example: In the natal chart of fraudulent hedge fund manager Bernie Madoff, Sun at 8 Taurus trines Ornamenta at 8 Virgo. He must have worked his schemes in order to surround himself with nice things.

ORPHEUS 3361

Discovery: April 24, 1982 by Carlos Torres.

Backstory: Orpheus was a gifted musician and singer who charmed the female population, the ancient Greek prototype of today's rock star. He had many admirers but was madly in love with Eurydice, whom he planned to marry. But tragically, on their wedding day Eurydice stepped on a snake in the grass, was bitten, and died.

Overcome with emotion, Orpheus entreated Hades, God of the Underworld, to release Eurydice back to him, and the two struck a deal: Orpheus could lead Eurydice back to the land of the living provided that he did not look behind at her.

Sadly, the pair encountered a dense patch of fog on their way out of the Underworld and Orpheus looked back to make sure Eurydice was still behind him. This innocent mistake cost him everything; Eurydice was once again banished to the Underworld, never to rejoin her beloved.

Orpheus was inconsolable but could not strike another deal to recover Eurydice. Noticing his grief, dozens of devoted maidens attempted to console him and attract him, but he disdained their efforts. The rejection caused a great deal of resentment and animosity among the women, who then took to angry pursuit of Orpheus across a field. They threw stones, branches, and whatever they could get their hands on in order to injure Orpheus, but nothing stopped him. Farmers who were tilling their fields nearby retreated from the violence, leaving their tools and instruments behind them, which the infuriated women were only to happy to take up in their pursuit.

Hell had no fury like these women scorned. Orpheus was no match for this assault by hoes (no pun intended), rakes, and sharp farming implements and he died on the scene, torn to bits by his pursuers. But only then was he was finally able to rejoin his beloved Eurydice in Hades for eternity.

Possible Interpretation: In the natal chart Orpheus can indicate a doomed relationship or self-sabotage; the loss of one is absolutely devastating to the other. Also indicative of a singer, poet, or one who is musically gifted; a rock star existence; an obsessive romantic nature; extreme grief over a loss.

Examples: In the natal chart of musician Kurt Cobain Orpheus at 25 Pisces conjoins Venus at 26 Pisces.

In the natal chart of Courtney Love, Cobain's wife at the time of his death and a fellow rock musician, Saturn at 4 Pisces squares Orpheus at 4 Gemini.

In the natal chart of singer/songwriter Gordon Lightfoot, Orpheus at 1 Aquarius trines his 0 degree Libra Moon.

Pop star/dancer/actress Jennifer Lopez has Mercury at 3 Leo trine Orpheus at 3 Aries.

Elvis the King had his 2 Pisces Moon in exact conjunction with Orpheus.

OSIRIS 1923

Discovery: September 24, 1960 by Ingrid and C. J. van Houten.

Backstory: Egyptian god of the dead and the underworld, the counterpart of the sun god Ra or Re. He is one of the most famous gods in the Egyptian pantheon. Born of Geb and Nut, he was the brother of Seth, Isis, and Nephthys. He is also associated with grain crops.

After his brother Seth murdered him and scattered his body parts, Isis conceived a child with his semen using a reconstructed phallus, and bore Horus. Subsequent rulers were considered the divine symbol of Horus in life and Osiris in death. He is also associated with Anubis, god of the dead and embalming. [see ANUBIS 1912]

Possible Interpretation: References rebirth and resurrection, having to undergo transformative experiences; association with death in some form; intense familial stress.

Examples: In the natal chart of kidnap/murder victim Charles Lindbergh, Jr., his Moon at 9 Taurus is partile opposite both Osiris and Cronos. There have long been suspicions that his father had some involvement in the boy's undoing.

Former President Bill Clinton has Mercury at 7 Leo square Dick at 8 Scorpio; his sexual misadventures are legend. His Mercury also conjoins Osiris.

OSTARA 343

Discovery: November 15, 1892 by Max Wolf.

B D SALERNO

Backstory: The Anglo-Saxon goddess of springtime, also known as Eostre in old German.

Possible Interpretation: Represents renewal, new beginnings, having a fresh start, youthfulness.

PABU 66652

Discovery: September 1999 by Chad Trujillo. TNO.

Backstory: Pabu is a twin to asteroid Borasisi, or binary; both are cubewanos. See BORASISI 66652. The names come from a novel by sci-fi writer Kurt Vonnegut, *Cat's Cradle,* in which they represent the Sun and the Moon.

Possible Interpretation: May symbolize a maverick, rebel, or forward thinker who breaks convention; someone with an awareness of higher consciousness, the collective, a broad thinker.

PAINE 5188

Discovery: October 15, 1990 by Eleanor F. Helin.

Backstory: Named after Thomas O. Paine (1921–1992), American metallurgist, third Administrator of NASA.

Possible Interpretation: I have noted a few diverse interpretations: a deep devotion to social causes; the drive to achieve justice; where we feel pain and distress, what pains us.

PALES 49

Discovery: September 19, 1857 by Hermann Goldschmidt, on the same night that he discovered Doris 48, almost naming the asteroid "the Twins".

Backstory: Roman goddess of shepherds, flocks, and livestock.

Possible Interpretation: Her festival is called Palilia or Parilia. May reference an affinity for raising animals or a business or practice involving animals, or one's tendency to manage or assist activities involving groups of individuals.

PALLAS 2

Discovery: March 28, 1802 by Heinrich Wilhelm Olbers.

Backstory: Only the second asteroid ever discovered, Pallas joins astrology's pantheon of the four main asteroids: Ceres, Pallas, Juno, and Vesta. Chiron did not come along until over a hundred years later, in 1977.

The Greek goddess Athena adopted the name Pallas Athena after accidentally killing her younger sister Pallas in a martial arts contest. Athena, daughter of Zeus from whose head she was born, is perhaps the most revered goddess in the Greek pantheon. She was skilled in war planning, justice, problem solving and negotiating. Her Roman counterpart is Minerva. See MINERVA 93.

Pallas is symbolized by the owl and the snake and also represents wisdom. Her gift to humanity was the olive, as the olive tree was sacred to her. As a respected warrior, she is often shown clad in goat skins with the head of the Gorgon Medusa on her breastplate.

Possible Interpretation: Depending on her placement in the horoscope she represents wisdom and intelligence; love of the fine arts; creativity; an excellent strategist; a political activist seeking justice. Pallas was also known for her sense of discipline and self-control, so afflictions to her asteroid may show the opposite.

Examples: Founder of the Red Cross, nurse Clara Barton had her Mars at 8 Virgo partile trine Pallas in Capricorn; she was heavily involved in saving lives during the Civil War and later conflicts.

B D SALERNO

In the natal chart of golf champion Tiger Woods, the Midheaven at 23 Gemini squares Pallas at 23 Pisces.

PANACEA 2878

Discovery: September 7, 1980 by Ed Bowell.

Backstory: Panacea is the daughter of Aesculapia, the great god of healing, the granddaughter of Apollo, the great granddaughter of Jupiter, and the sister of Hygeia, so she represents an illustrious bloodline.

Possible Interpretation: A panacea is something to make things better, which connects to her healing abilities. It is what we do to improve an ailing situation. Sometimes it is not always for the better; it may also show where we try to improve things by covering up, self-medicating, and other forms of avoidance, as there is a delusional aspect to this quality.

I have noted this asteroid featured strongly in crime charts where the victim was impaired by drink or drugs, their panacea out of a difficult situation or troublesome feelings. The asteroid Panacea relates to this as well.

Examples: In the natal chart of serial killer Edmund Kemper, Panacea at 6 Pisces is partile opposite Saturn. He felt driven to commit the killings to relieve his deeply ingrained fear of rejection by women.

In the natal chart of 1950s actress Jean Seberg, her 29 Libra Ascendant directly opposes Panacea. Depressed and hounded by various agencies, she died of an overdose of drugs.

In the natal chart of Marshall Applewhite, founder of the suicidal religious group Heaven's Gate, Jupiter at 17 Cancer partile trines

Panacea in Scorpio. In 1997 his 39 followers all drank poison so that their souls could be reunited in space travel with the Hale-Bopp comet.

Beach Boys musician Dennis Wilson had Mercury at 4 Capricorn partile opposite Panacea; he struggled with alcohol and drug addiction and drowned at the age of 39.

PANDORA 55

Discovery: September 10, 1858 by George Searle.

Backstory: It is a large, bright asteroid, as well as a moon of Saturn. The asteroid was named following a dispute between two women, one the widow of the owner of Dudley Observatory in Albany, New York, and another astronomer.

Possible interpretation: The gods sent a box to Pandora that she wasn't supposed to open, but of course she opened it, releasing mayhem and madness that rapidly spread throughout the world. Opening a Pandora's box is a metaphor for unintentionally creating or discovering a chaotic circumstance that gets out of hand (unless you have a cat named Pandora, in which case her box contains litter and other unpleasant items).

Curiosity brings consequences, as can reckless behavior with little forethought, and hopefully, learning from past mistakes. Poking around where we shouldn't is also a possible meaning for this asteroid.

Examples: Adolf Eichmann, one of Hitler's top Nazi henchmen who helped plan the extermination of Jews, had his 28 Pisces Sun exactly conjunct Pandora. He was executed by hanging in Israel in 1962.

In the natal chart of occultist and rocket scientist Jack Parson, founder of the Jet Propulsion Laboratory, Mars at 2 Scorpio forms a partile square to Pandora. He accidentally blew himself up during an experiment, a box he should not have tampered with.

J. Robert Oppenheimer, "father of the atomic bomb," had his 23 Cancer Moon in partile trine to both Pandora and Ceto in Pisces.

PANOPAEA 70

Discovery: May 5, 1861 by Robert Luther.

Backstory: A nymph in Greek mythology whom sailors invoked during difficult or stormy sea voyages. One of the 50 nereids born of Nereus and Doris.

Possible Interpretation: May show someone who is helpful during a crisis, or whether the person would be supportive if called upon in a time of distress.

Example: In the natal chart of Japanese artist Yoko Ono, wife of musician John Lennon, her 29 Aquarius Sun squares Panopaea at 29 Scorpio.

PARIS 3317

Discovery: May 26, 1984 by Carolyn and Eugene Shoemaker.

Backstory: Prince Paris was one of the sons of King Priam of Troy and Queen Hecuba. Before his birth it was prophesied that he would cause a disastrous war, which he did by abducting the wife of King Menelaus of Sparta, the beautiful Helen, which caused the Trojan War. Although Helen was married, Aphrodite promised her hand to Paris, and he would not heed warnings against taking her for himself.

The matter was complicated further by Eros, who fired a love arrow into the heart of Helen when she first set eyes on Paris. She was immediately smitten and the two quickly ran off together, setting the bloody war in motion.

During the war Paris killed Achilles by firing an arrow into his heel, the only part of his body that was vulnerable to injury. The Greeks were devastated by his loss, so in retaliation Paris was slain by one of Heracles' poisoned arrows.

Possible Interpretation: Asteroid Paris indicates boldness, courage, and daring; the drive to pursue one's desires at any cost. However, as the story went, chasing one's passions hell-bent against the advice of others can cause many repercussions. Impetuousness and rash judgment are also indicated especially if the asteroid is afflicted.

Example: In the natal chart of Super Bowl champion quarterback Tom Brady, his 11 Leo Sun squares Paris at 12 Taurus.

PART 4087

Discovery: March 5, 1986 by Edward Bowell.

Backstory: Not found.

Possible Interpretation: Departure, what we move away from or part with; in crime astrology, may represent a part of something, as evidence.

PARTHENOPE 11

Discovery: May 11, 1850 by Annibale de Gasparis.

Backstory: The name means "maiden-voiced," and appropriately, she was a Greek siren. She was attracted to Odysseus, but he rejected her advances. Unable to overcome the rejection, she drowned herself.

Possible Interpretation: May reference where we have trouble dealing with rejection; where we go overboard (no pun intended) in our desire for a particular person or thing, or where we put too much energy into a one-sided situation; a desire to hitch one's wagon to a star, to have high expectations (which, in Pathenope's case, were not met).

PECKER 1629

Discovery: February 28, 1952 by Louis Boyer.

Backstory: Named after Dr. Jean-Claude Pecker. As we have seen, the slang name has its own resonance to the asteroid, as I have noted in some online analyses and some of my own.

Possible Interpretation: Unfortunately, this asteroid has been designated a whole other meaning for the male phallus, and with all due respect to Dr. Pecker, this weirdly bears out.

This is not the only time a name has acquired dual significance, as we will shortly see with PREVERT 18624. This generally tends to happen with named asteroids, where a person's name can take on dual meanings.

Examples: Ted Bundy, prolific serial killer of over 33 women, had Pecker at 10 Aquarius partile conjunct Ceres and partile trine Neptune in Libra.

Serial murderer Dennis Rader ("BTK Killer") has his Pecker at 3 Cancer partile conjunct Saturn, which must be uncomfortable indeed.

In the natal chart of the "Bay Area Rapist" Joseph DeAngelo, Apophis at 26 Aries trines his Sun at 26 Sagittarius and opposes his Venus at 25 Libra (which conjoins his Pecker at 24 Libra).

ASTEROIDS OUR COSMIC INFLUENCERS

British serial murderer Dennis Nilsen, a gay man who savagely murdered gay men whom he enticed to his apartment, had Mars at 2 Leo square Pecker at 2 Scorpio.

In the natal chart of Branch Davidian founder David Koresh, Swindle at 7 Taurus forms a square to Mercury at 7 Leo, while Pecker at 7 Scorpio fits into a t-square; he slept with his female followers, regardless of their marital status, including teenagers. His was more devoted to the yearnings of Pecker than to the teachings of Christ.

PEITHO 118

Discovery: March 15, 1872 by Robert Luther.

Backstory: Greek goddess of persuasion and seduction.

Possible Interpretation: An understanding of how to get one's way; how to manipulate others; good at sales, politics and other trades that require persuasive skills.

Example: Felonious hedge fund manager Bernie Madoff, with his 4 Gemini Mars in trine to Peitho at 4 Aquarius, convinced dozens of wealthy investors that they could get even richer by investing in his fraudulent funds.

PELION 49038

Discovery: August 21, 1998 by David J. Tholen[5] and Robert J. Whiteley[6]. TNO.

---

5. https://www.google.com/
search?sca_esv=3c150c50f502bc5d&sca_upv=1&hl=en&gbv=2&sxsrf=ADLYWIL4GOpYD6UcBwaUi9cvN7soY7rEmA:1726694185875&q=David+J.+Tholen&si=ACC90nzx_D3_zUKRnpAjmO0UBLNxnt7EyN4YYdru6U3bxLI-LwYKjhY1blXZntmVLEIsmJtu2ACnggg-XlS1R9pNjdqJOzCpUaliyu9XR71UsyF-8c7Xdu27LS3JbjtTGzndIxIUyKhJ2H-OCAD-tlNg3FlZob7s5_CaaT-OBxDOL5T4hNbewipz-7_6aJqNwkHa-

B D SALERNO

Backstory: Pelion was the name of the mountain home of the healing centaur Chiron.

Possible Interpretation: Mountains require steep climbs, as this asteroid represents in the horoscope where we face huge obstacles, where we are required to dig deep down for the stamina to overcome it. Chiron had a wounded knee, so the mountain presented an almost insurmountable task to climb, but he managed to live there, having figured out how to navigate it.

Example: Booker T. Washington, African-American writer, educator, and activist, had Jupiter at 29 Pisces square Pelion at 29 Gemini; as a black man during the early 20th Century he faced and overcame numerous obstacles in establishing educational protocols and institutions for fellow black Americans.

In the natal chart of activist/attorney Robert F. Kennedy, Jr., Mercury at 29 Capricorn partile opposes Pelion. He suffers from spasmodic dysphonia which affects his speaking voice.

PENTHESILEA 271

Hjisi2ahxxH9YsOHRPksHzs97Inkb0SOqoFzR_Z17cvc-Z63OrarydXUp08oWrvIkqSM5fQ&sa=X&ved=2ahUKEwiGmtaMtc2IAxWArokEHcbrGGAQmxN6BAgMEAo

6. https://www.google.com/search?sca_esv=3c150c50f502bc5d&sca_upv=1&hl=en&gbv=2&sxsrf=ADLYWIL4GOpYD6UcBwaUi9cvN7soY7rEmA:1726694185875&q=Robert+J.+Whiteley&si=ACC90nwLLwns5sISZcdzuISy7t-NHozt8Cbt6G3WNQfC9ekAgEimBs1-r0HVSFbCUQVKwt93jXXZzYvTuzPsfcHQiGRbdUaQkJq3hJKs4jQiGTJhwSKzHNhsWV-ZhnHbDtXJsfX9esMylj0qfNHq9o6SJxWW5VvLJ4zyaKu8coBRSxfYD06tnO9D4_6oz2ZYwKUnxQDIm0zOobCa4CrBC3SAS27pk6zRIi7TYxCGg0pqH4H4S_YKbdwvOfXkX6KpSJ_WrXGVCzNIddk6odhKkxobw5EeSlB1FQ%3D%3D&sa=X&ved=2ahUKEwiGmtaMtc2IAxWArokEHcbrGGAQmxN6BAgMEAs

ASTEROIDS OUR COSMIC INFLUENCERS

Discovery: October 13, 1887 by Victor Knorre.

Backstory: An Amazon queen and great woman warrior; see also AMAZONE 1042 and HIPPOLYTA 10295.

Possible Interpretation: A person of physical strength, possibly of large or tall size; someone who dominates and does not submit to men; feminist or women's rights supporter; female athlete or extremely competitive person.

Example: In the natal chart of tennis superstar Serena Williams, Venus at 16 Scorpio opposes Penthesile at 17 Taurus.

PERSEPHONE 399

Discovery: February 23, 1895 by Max Wolf.

Backstory: Persephone was the Greek goddess of the Underworld. She was known as Proserpina to the Romans, and has a separate asteroid by this name.

The daughter of Zeus, Persephone was extremely beautiful, but spurned her suitors because of her attachment to her mother; the two were inseparable. But she was lusted after by Zeus' brother, her uncle Hades.

Unconcerned about any ill effects to his own daughter, Zeus allowed Hades to kidnap Persephone and spirit her off to his underground kingdom where he made her an unwilling Queen of the Underworld. She immediately stopped eating as a result of the trauma.

However, Persephone ruled over grain and corn as a goddess of agriculture on Earth. During planting season she was sorely missed, as farmers needed her assistance in growing and harvesting their crops. She was ultimately allowed to remain 'topside' as it were except for the three months of winter when she had to reside in Hades.

In one version of this myth Persephone willingly went into the Underworld with the dark and sexy Hades, but by most reliable accounts this is not true.

Possible Interpretation: References kidnapping, rape, sexual abuse; PTSD as a result of trauma; addictions; eating disorders; where we feel we have been taken captive and not allowed to be ourselves; involvement with a coercive spouse. Also references some connection with death or the underworld; confinement or imprisonment; agricultural activities, farming.

Examples: In the natal chart of canonized saint Mother Teresa, Persephone is partile conjunct Venus at 8 Leo. She traveled the world over caring for the sick and dying, and spent most of her time exposed to death and extreme suffering.

The whole world knew of Princess Diana's sadness due to her unhappy marriage to Prince Charles. She had Sun at 9 Cancer trine Persephone at 9 Pisces.

In the natal chart of kidnap victim Elizabeth Smart, her 17 Aries Moon partile squares Persephone. She was returned to her family after spending 18 months with her disturbed kidnapper's family.

Nelson Mandela, South Africa's first democratically elected President, had Mars at 12 Libra trine Persephone at 12 Aquarius; he had been imprisoned for 27 years due to his anti-apartheid views.

Cesar Chavez, activist who defended the rights of immigrant workers, had Persephone at 4 Virgo conjunct his 3 Virgo Midheaven. The workers were migrants who picked fruits and vegetables in the fields.

PEST 6817

Discovery: January 20, 1982 by Antonin Mrkos.

Backstory: Named for the beautiful Hungarian city of Pest, which combines with its other half, Buda, to form Budapest.

Possible Interpretation: As it sounds, may refer to Hungary or Budapest, or a person or item with a Hungarian connection or interest. Alternately, may be what irritates us, what gets in our way; a nuisance.

PHAEDRA 174

Discovery: September 2, 1877 by James Craig Watson.

Backstory: Named after a tragic lovelorn queen in Greek mythology, the daughter of King Minos of Crete and wife of Theseus. Her name derives from the Greek word for "bright," although her love life was anything but.

One day she was struck by an arrow from Eros (Cupid) while gazing upon the youthful, handsome Hippolytus, her own stepson. She fell madly in love with him, but struggled with her emotions; after all, he was her husband's son and a young man who prided himself on his virginity and purity. Phaedra's angst drove her to confide in her nurse, who unfortunately let the cat out of the bag, spilling the tea on none other than Hippolytus himself. Phaedra's feelings of shame and disgrace led her to take her own life.

But that wasn't all. Before she died Phaedra left a letter accusing Hippolytus of seducing her, which resulted in a dumpster fire of family intrigues and the banishment and near death of Hippolytus. In her last moments she struck back in vengeance at her beloved - and it worked.

Possible Interpretation: References sorrow through loss of love; unrequited love with consequences; involvement in painful love triangles or inappropriate love situations; spitefulness and hostile retribution.

Examples: Princess Beatrice of York has Mercury at 22 Leo partile opposite Phaedra; she has endured many difficulties with heartbreak and hostile media.

PHAEO 322

Discovery: November 27, 1891 by Alphonse Borrelly.

Backstory: One of the numerous Greek Hyades or nymphs; she was tasked with providing rain.

Possible Interpretation: The connection to rain suggests that she is associated with grief or crying; also, providing water as nourishment and sustenance. May show where we need emotional "irrigation," or the release of grievous emotions.

PHAETHON 3200

Discovery: October 11, 1983 by the Infrared Astronomical Satellite.

Backstory: Phaethon, born to the Sun God, Helius, asked his father's permission to drive the chariot of the sun – but being an exuberant youth, he drove the chariot recklessly, causing injury and damage all around. He was taking on a task that was too big for him, and he quickly lost control of it. Zeus finally struck him down with a lightning bolt in order to save the lives of others.

Possible Interpretation: References where we bite off more than we can chew, often with disastrous consequences; reckless activity; where we lose control of situations and overestimate our ability to accomplish something.

Examples: Phaethon also represents vehicles themselves (chariots) and is prominently shown in the birth charts of NASCAR champion Kyle Petty and British Formula One champion Jackie Stewart who, during races, drive extremely fast and must take great care not to lose control of their vehicles.

In the natal chart of Adolf Hitler, the Sun at 0 Taurus exactly conjoins Phaethon. As World War II progressed he became increasingly reckless in his battle strategies, ultimately costing him control of his forces and eventual defeat. By invading Russia he was biting off way more than his beleaguered army could chew.

In the crime chart of Diane Downs, who killed two of her three children in order to appease a boyfriend who did not want children, Mars (gunfire) is strongly configured to Phaethon (vehicle); she shot her three children while they were seated in her car. It can't get more literal than that.

French serial killer Henri Landru had Phaethon at 12 Taurus partile conjunct Jupiter; his method was strangulation (Venus, ruler of Taurus, rules the throat). He was eventually caught and executed by guillotine.

In the natal chart of Mafia boss John Gotti, his 19 Virgo Moon partile opposes Phaethon; his murderous takedown of the previous "capo" was audacious and daring, but his sidekick, Sammy Gravano, betrayed him in the end.

Chicago mob boss Al Capone had his 27 Capricorn Sun exactly conjoined to Phaethon; Mars was not too far ahead at 29 Capricorn.

Controversial Youtuber Logan Paul has Mars at 13 Leo in partile trine to both Phaethon and Hermes at 13 Aries.

PHAETUSA 296

Discovery: August 19, 1890 by Auguste Charlois.

Backstory: A Greek goddess renowned for great beauty and charm.

B D SALERNO

Possible Interpretation: May indicate beauty and charisma, especially if configured to the Ascendant; shows qualities that express a level of attractiveness or charm, be it physical or social.

Examples: In the natal chart of supermodel Cindy Crawford, Phaetusa at 3 Sagittarius exactly trines her Aries Midheaven.

Supermodel Naomi Campbell has her Mercury at 13 Taurus sextile Phaetusa at 13 Pisces.

PHOLUS 5145

Discovery: January 9, 1992 by David Rabinowitz. Centaur.

Backstory: Pholus is an "eccentric centaur" crossing the orbits of Saturn and Neptune. Mythological centaur son of Cronus and Philyra, and companion of Hercules; he fell on an arrow and died while hunting. It was Pholus who tried to rescue fellow centaur Nessus who was shot with a poisoned arrow by Helius while in the act of assaulting Helius' wife Dejaneira.

Possible Interpretation: May symbolize trying to correct or save a desperate situation; the person may have skills in fixing broken things by putting the pieces back together, either literally or figuratively; needing to fix problems.

Examples: L. Ron Hubbard, founder of the Church of Scientology, had Jupiter at 14 Scorpio partile conjunct Pholus; his methodology was intended to appeal to people seeking an answer to their problems.

In the natal chart of President-elect Donald Trump, whose first campaign promised to "drain the swamp," his Venus at 25 Cancer opposes Pholus at 24 Capricorn.

PHOTOGRAPHICA 443

ASTEROIDS OUR COSMIC INFLUENCERS

Discovery: February 27, 1899 by Max Wolf.

Backstory: Max Wolf was a well-known German astronomer who was the first to develop a system of photographing asteroids with the use of camera lenses.

Possible Interpretation: A talent for photography and optics; using photography or optics in one's career; being the subject of photography, as a model or celebrity.

Examples: J. Edgar Hoover, head of the FBI for many decades, had his 3 Scorpio Midheaven opposite Photographica at 2 Taurus; his agents often photographed subjects who were under surveillance and used the photos for purposes of blackmail. Ironically, he too was photographed in compromising positions by the Mafia, and throughout his career he emphatically denied their existence.

Popular TV psychologist Dr. Joyce Brothers had her 17 Capricorn Moon in exact trine to Photographica at 17 Virgo. She was very well known through her many appearances on talk television shows and in the print media.

Hollywood producer and convicted rapist Harvey Weinstein has Mercury at 17 Aries in partile opposition to Photographica.

In the natal chart of actor/director/producer Clint Eastwood, Jupiter at 24 II forms a square to Photographica at 23 Pisces.

PINOCCHIO 12927

Discovery: September 30, 1999 by Maura Tombelli and Luciano Tesi.

Backstory: Named for the colorful fictional Italian character Pinocchio, whose nose grew longer every time he told a lie. The book *The Adventures of Pinocchio* was written in 1883 by Carlo Collodi and immortalized in the 1940 Disney movie "Pinocchio".

The book tells the story of an old man, Ser Geppetto, who is lonely and fashions himself a marionette out of sculpted wood. The puppet comes to life as the young boy that Geppetto always wanted, but becomes abusive to Geppetto, lying and cheating. It's a dark story, and interesting that early Disney gave it life in a feature-length animation.

Possible Interpretation: Where we engage in make-believe, fantasy, spinning tall tales; telling lies; giving life to a fantasy that becomes a monster.

Example: Former President and Army General Dwight D. Eisenhower had Mars at 13 Capricorn partile conjunct Pinocchio. His famous speech about the dangers of the military industrial complex, which he was a part of for many years, serves as a wake-up call to those who placed so much trust in the system.

PLUTO-CHARON 134340

Discovery: June 1978 by James Christy and Robert Harrington. Dwarf Planet.

Backstory: Charon is the largest of Pluto's five moons, Charon being half the size of Pluto and therefore the largest known satellite in regard to its parent planet. Charon is the ferryman of dead souls to the realm of the Underworld, or Hades, in Greek mythology. His Roman counterpart is Pluto.

Possible Interpretation: Interesting to note that the five moons of Pluto are named Hades, Styx, Nix, Kerberus, and Charon, all relating to death, transition, and transformation, so it's safe to interpret that this asteroid refers the individual to an interest, obsession, or profession involving these activities.

Examples: In the nativity of politician Hillary Clinton, Mars at 14 Leo partile conjoins Pluto-Charon.

ASTEROIDS OUR COSMIC INFLUENCERS

Former Iraqi dictator Saddam Hussein had Jupiter at 26 Capricorn in partile opposition to Pluto-Charon; he was tried and executed by hanging.

In the natal chart of kidnap victim Elizabeth Smart, her Sun at 10 Scorpio conjoined Pluto-Charon at 9 Scorpio. After eighteen months in captivity she was safely returned to her family.

In the natal chart of 1950s actress Jean Seberg, Venus at 1 Sagittarius forms a partile trine to Pluto-Charon in Leo. She was under surveillance by government agencies because of her political leanings. The constant fear and harassment, coupled with the death of her daughter, drove her to take her own life.

Occultist and rocket scientist Jack Parsons, who founded the Jet Propulsion Laboratory, had his 1 Scorpio Mercury partile conjunct Atropos, and conjunct Apophis at 1 Scorpio, forming a trine with his Saturn-Pluto-Charon conjunction in Cancer. Venus at 2 Scorpio also fits in here. He accidentally blew himself up during a lab experiment.

In the natal chart of singer Whitney Houston, Venus at 11 Leo partile conjoins Pluto-Charon; her death by accidental drowning in a bathtub, while under the influence of drugs, has long been considered suspicious.

In the natal chart of horror movie director Wes Craven, Venus at 0 Leo is conjunct Pluto-Charon at 1 Leo.

POISSON 12874

Discovery: August 19, 1998 by Paul G. Comba.

Backstory: Named after influential French mathematician, teacher and scholar Siméon Denis Poisson. Poisson also means "fish" in French.

Possible Interpretation: Since poisson resembles the word poison, some astrologers have noted it in crime charts where drugs were involved. I venture a guess that it could reference a scholarly teacher like Poisson, or something to do with fish, or even poisonous materials or drugs. It is well worth looking further into this asteroid to get a fix on what it may reveal; I have come up with a few examples below.

Examples: In the natal chart of Marshall Applewhite, founder of the suicidal religious group Heaven's Gate, the North Node at 13 Aries conjoins Poisson. In 1997 his 39 followers all drank poison so that their souls could be reunited in space travel with the Hale-Bopp comet.

Judy Buenoano, a.k.a the "Black Widow," was the first woman executed in Florida. In 1971 she killed her husband by poisoning him. In her chart Mars at 20 Aquarius was conjunct Amor at 21, both opposed by Poisson at 21 Leo.

Notorious drug trafficker Pablo Escobar's natal chart showed complex inter-relationships with Poisson at 24 Capricorn: Venus at 25 Capricorn, Elatus at 25 Capricorn, Vesta at 25 Capricorn, all in square to Moon at 25 Aries, which also formed a trine to Zeus at 25 Leo.

Church of Scientology founder L. Ron Hubbard had Mars at 29 Capricorn partile conjoined to Poisson; he drank heavily and took drugs, and as a member of the Navy, also enjoyed sailing. He was expelled from the Navy for taking illicit gunnery practice by firing into the ocean off the coast of Mexico.

POLYHYMNIA 33

Discovery: October 28, 1854 by Jean Chacomac.

Backstory: Greek Muse of singing, especially sacred and religious music and dancing.

ASTEROIDS OUR COSMIC INFLUENCERS

Example: Christian rock singer Amy Grant's Polyhymnia at 4 Capricorn conjuncts her Jupiter at 5 Capricorn.

POMONA 32

Discovery: October 26, 1854 by Hermann Goldschmidt.

Backstory: Roman goddess of fruit trees, orchards, gardens, and the seasons of plant growth; comes from the Latin word for fruit, "pomum."

Possible Interpretation: Represents interest or hobbies in these areas, or the joy of cultivating life.

Example: In the natal chart of Booker T. Washington, African-American writer, educator, and activist, Mercury at 23 Aries is trine Pomona at 24 Leo. He promoted agricultural pursuits, especially gardening, as a way toward gaining self-sufficiency and self-esteem.

POMPEJA 203

Discovery: September 25, 1879 by Christian Peters.

Backstory: Pompeii, southern Italian city destroyed by earthquake in 79 CE. Several sites are still being excavated today.

Possible Interpretation: May indicate where things are suddenly altered by circumstances beyond our control, where we experience a devastating change and the need to rebuild.

Example: In the natal chart of tennis champion Martina Navratilova, Moon at 12 Aries partile conjoins Pompeja. In 2023 she announced that she was cancer-free after undergoing treatments for breast and throat cancer.

B D SALERNO

POSEIDON 4341

Discovery: May 29, 1987 by Carolyn Shoemaker.

Backstory: There is also a Uranian planet named Poseidon. I have not found significant differences in the interpretations, as they both refer to the same mythological deity.

As the son of the titans Cronos and Rhea, his brothers were Zeus and Hades, and the three of them ruled the earth, underworld, and the seas, respectively, with the three sharing the earth. Poseidon is one of the most powerful of the twelve Olympians. He is the god of the sea, earthquakes, horses, and his Roman counterpart is Neptune.

Possible Interpretation: Poseidon rules the ocean depths, where we are into a situation way over our heads; we can only sense and feel but not see our way out; may convey a spiritually high side, or Neptune's flip side of deception, disillusionment, and dissipation. May also show an interest in oceanography, travel by sea, and deeper states of consciousness.

Example: In the natal chart of Monica Lewinsky, who had a very public affair with President Bill Clinton in the White House, has Mars at 20 Aries opposite Poseidon at 20 Libra.

PRAAMZIUS 420356

Discovery: January 23, 2012 by Kazimieras Czernis. TNO.

Backstory: Named for the Lithuanian god of the sky.

Possible Interpretation: Relates to changes in perception after a dramatic, possibly life-altering, event.

ASTEROIDS OUR COSMIC INFLUENCERS

Examples: In the natal chart of German tennis star Steffi Graf, the 14 Gemini Moon conjoins Praamzius at 13 Gemini. She has had to cope with the tragedy of losing her daughter in a car crash since June 2024.

Celebrity Oprah Winfrey, who has publicly shared traumatic events of her past, has Mars at 23 Scorpio in opposition to Praamzius at 22 Taurus.

PREVERT 18624

Discovery: Not available.

Backstory: Data was not available, and this is appropriate for this asteroid, as it has been described alternately as the name of a French writer, Prevert, but also interpreted as "Pervert."

Possible Interpretation: It's interesting to note that I have seen instances where the "pervert" designation was suitable in a crime chart and in those cases it referred to criminal and unconventional sexual behavior.

Example: British serial killer Dennis Nilsen, a gay man who murdered his gay male sex partners, had Uranus at 16 Gemini square Prevert at 17 Pisces.

PREY 6157

Discovery: September 9, 1991 by Lutz D. Schmadel and Freimut Börngen.

Backstory: Named after Adalbert Prey, professor of astronomy at the University of Innsbruck in Austria.

Possible Interpretation: May be literal, having to do with the professor, someone named Prey, or a connection with the university or

Austria. Many astrologers also interpret it to mean feeling overmatched or bullied; in a crime chart may show bullying or stalking.

PROMETHEUS 1809

Discovery: September 24, 1960 by C. J. van Houten.

Backstory: Called "the Bringer of Fire," he was son of Iapetus and Clymene, Titans whose rule he disapproved of, and he became a supporter of Zeus and the Olympians after the Titans were dethroned.

Later on the two gods had a falling out over the dispensation of meat as food among the humans and gods – the humans got the better part while the gods got the scraps. Zeus wasn't happy with scraps so he chained Prometheus to a rock, consigned to have his liver pecked out by an eagle. Somewhat inconveniently, the liver would grow back just in time to be consumed by the eagle again. But Prometheus had aided Heracles with one of his Twelve Labors and to return the favor Heracles unchained him from the rock. He was later forgiven by Zeus.

Possible Interpretation: Prometheus symbolizes areas of life where the person is out of harmony with friends and family, feels literally caught between a rock and a hard place where following authority is concerned, or feels tortured by circumstances.

PROSERPINA 26

Discovery: May 5, 1853 by Robert Luther.

See PERSEPHONE 399 above; Proserpina is the Roman version of Persephone.

PSYCHE 16

Discovery: March 17, 1852 by Annibale de Gasparis.

ASTEROIDS OUR COSMIC INFLUENCERS

Backstory: A metal rich asteroid, it is called Psyche in both Greek and Roman mythology.

Goddess of the soul in Greek mythology; born human, she married Eros (Cupid), god of love and sexual passion. Being human, she was not allowed to gaze upon her husband, but stole a glance by candlelight. When hot wax dripped onto Eros he became angry and flew away.

Eros' mother Aphrodite punished her by giving her four tasks, the fourth of which was difficult to complete – to steal Aphrodite's beauty cream (good heavens!). She managed to open the jar but then fell into a deathly sleep, as wily Aphrodite had drugged the cream.

Almost as stunningly beautiful as Aphrodite, Psyche was eventually granted immortality and is depicted as a woman with butterfly wings.

Possible Interpretation: Psyche may refer to the study of the psychology of the mind, the emotions, the drive for love and passion. Afflictions may indicate emotional or psychological issues.

Examples: In the natal chart of serial rapist/killer/cannibal Jeffrey Dahmer, Psyche at 2 Taurus grand trines his Jupiter at 2 Capricorn and Pluto at 3 Virgo.

Julian Assange has Mercury at 24 Cancer in exact conjunction to Psyche.

Controversial Youtube celebrity Logan Paul has Sun at 11 Aries conjunct Psyche at 10.

In the natal chart of Hollywood producer and convicted rapist Harvey Weinstein, Venus at 4 Pisces makes multiple contacts in exact opposition to Dziewanna, Psyche, and Diana, and sextiles Dick at 4 Capricorn, which exactly conjoins Salacia.

B D SALERNO

Michael Aquino, Lieutenant Colonel of Psychological Operations, US Army, and founder of the Tempe of Set, had Venus at 0 Sagittarius in exact square to Psyche at 0 Virgo. Venus also trined Pandora at 0 Leo.

PYGMALION 96189

Discovery: July 6, 1991 by Henri Debehogne.

Backstory: Pygmalion was a legendary king of Cyprus and grandfather to Adonis. In a chart he represents man's need to transform a woman into someone of his liking.

The story of Pygmalion is told in the famous musical/movie "My Fair Lady," in which the lead male character meets a crude, uneducated street urchin and gradually transforms her into an educated, refined member of society.

Possible Interpretation: It is about transformation from a crude and unrefined nature to that of a polished and socially acceptable personality; describes a situation in which someone tries to make over someone else, either by influence or coercion; grooming for transformation.

Example: In the natal chart of celebrity Sean Combs, a.k.a. "P. Diddy," Venus at 22 Libra partile trines Pygmalion in Aquarius; evidence relating to sex trafficking, sexual abuse, and grooming of women for exploitation has recently landed him in jail.

PYTHIA 432

Discovery: December 18, 1897 by Auguste Charlois.

Backstory: Pythia was the Greek high priestess who channeled prophetic messages from Apollo at the Oracle of Delphi.

Possible Interpretation: She symbolizes a highly intuitive individual, a seer, psychic or one with divining skills; someone who is good at interpreting signals in the behavior or communication of others, or omens.

Example: Medical intuitive/author/lecturer Caroline Myss has Venus at 20 Capricorn opposite Pythia at 21 Cancer.

QUAOAR 50000

Discovery: June 4, 2002 by Michael E. Brown and Chad Trujillo. Dwarf Planet.

Backstory: Like Borasisi, a cubewano, non-resonant to any planet; it is also a dwarf planet. It is pronounced KWA-war, a Native American deity of creation.

Possible Interpretation: The celestial bodies that operate beyond the orbit of Neptune, nearer to Pluto, are also known as Plutoids or Ice Dwarf Planets.

In this case, Quaoar represents an energy that is dynamically creative and innovative, signifying one who thinks or acts outside the box with a uniquely individual perspective, which can be positive if well aspected. If poorly aspected it can sometimes border on egotism and self-serving motives.

Examples: In the natal chart of Jeffrey Epstein, his Moon at 10 Aries is opposite Quaoar at 11 Libra. With his ravenous appetite for underage girls he certainly broke from societal convention, doing his own thing until he was finally arrested and incarcerated.

Theoretical physicist J. Robert Oppenheimer, "father of the atomic bomb," had Venus at 11 Aries in trine to Quaoar at 10 Leo.

QUETZALCOHUATL 1915

B D SALERNO

Discovery: March 9, 1953 by Albert George Wilson.

Backstory: A Mesoamerican god of Aztec times, from the 1300s through the 1500s.

He was identified with the morning and evening star, similar to Venus. He ruled over many things: the priesthood, craftsmen, books, and the calendar. Most importantly, he was associated with death and transformation. He was accompanied by a Xolotl, a dog-headed god reminiscent of Anubis with his jackal head. The two would bring back the bones of the dead and anoint them with blood to give birth to new life in the world.

Possible Interpretation: The asteroid represents transformation through crisis, the hope for resurrection, and endings; also, skills associated with crafts, tradesmen, specialized knowledge, and measurements of time.

RA-SHALOM 2100

Discovery: September 10, 1978 by Eleanor Kay Helin.

Backstory: The asteroid's name is a combination of Ra, the Egyptian Sun God, and Shalom, the Hebrew word and greeting meaning "peace." It was named during the Camp David peace accord meetings between Egypt and Israel.

Possible Interpretation: Where we seek peaceful resolution of internal or external conflicts on a physical or emotional level.

Example: In the natal chart of medical intuitive/author/lecturer Caroline Myss, Mars at 8 Aquarius conjoins Ra-Shalom at 9, which is also sextiled by her Sun at 10 Sagittarius.

REQUIEM 2254

ASTEROIDS OUR COSMIC INFLUENCERS

Discovery: Discovered August 19, 1977 by Nikolai Chernykh.

Backstory: The asteroid was named for the high funeral mass because the astronomer Chernykh's mother passed away on the day of the asteroid's discovery.

Possible Interpretation: Relates to funeral mass or burial; passing of someone; change, transformation, death of the ego, posthumous honors.

Examples: Famed nurse Florence Nightingale, who served the wounded and dying during the Crimean War, had her natal Sun-Moon conjunction at 21 and 22 Taurus in partile conjunction to Requiem.

In the natal chart of Nazi official Adolf Eichmann, Mercury at 16 Aries ezactly conjoins Requiem. He was instrumental in plotting the "final solution" of the Jews during World War II.

RHADAMANTHUS 38083

Discovery: April 17, 1999 by the Deep Ecliptic Survey at Kitt Peak Observatory. Centaur.

Backstory: As the son of Zeus and Europa, Rhadamanthus was gifted with wisdom, and after his death he was made judge of the Underworld, where he determined punishments for all those who came before him.

Possible Interpretation: Shows where we may be judged or called into account for our actions, possibly requiring change and adaptation.

Examples: Rock star Courtney Love has Mercury at 1 Leo partile conjunct Rhadamanthus.

Politician Hillary Clinton has her 28 Pisces Moon partile conjunct Rhadamanthus.

B D SALERNO

Heavyweight boxing champion Muhammad Ali has Mercury at 13 Aquarius in partile trine to Rhadamanthus, which also formed a sextile to Amycus at 13 Aries.

RHIPHONOS 346889

Discovery: August 28, 2009 by Timur V. Kryachko. Centaur.

Backstory: The name means 'throwing'; the meaning may relate to being cast into a task and having to perform it.

Possible Interpretation: Represents things we throw ourselves into with conviction, or where we are compelled to do something; situations we are thrown into.

Examples: In the natal chart of pop star Madonna, Venus at 0 Leo exactly squares Rhiphonos at 0 Scorpio.

In the natal chart of Scientology founder L. Ron Hubbard, Rhiphonos at 13 Virgo opposes his 14 Pisces Moon.

RUSSIA 232

Discovery: January 31, 1883 by Johann Palisa.

Backstory: Named after the country.

Possible Interpretation: References the country, travel thereto or interest in the culture, history, language; connection by ancestry or circumstances.

Examples: In the natal chart of actress Natalie Wood, her Moon at 0 Taurus is partile conjunct Russia. She was of Russian heritage; her birth name was Natalia Nikolaevna Zakharenko.

ASTEROIDS OUR COSMIC INFLUENCERS

Actor Kirk Douglas had Mars at 5 Capricorn partile conjunct Russia; he too was of Russian descent, with a birth name of Issur Danielovitch Demsky.

SADO 118230

Discovery: November 30, 1996 by Nâoto Satō.

Backstory: Like Prevert, this seems to be one of those asteroids that has taken on a life outside of that which may have been intended.

Possible Interpretation: References aggressive behavior, sado-masochism or a sadistic temperament, especially if afflicted; sadness or depression, emotional maladjustment.

Example: David Koresh, the charismatic founder of the Branch Davidian religious sect, had his Sun at 24 Leo in square to Sado at 25 Scorpio. He helped himself to having sexual relations with his female followers, regardless of their marital status, taunting their husbands into allowing this coercion.

SALACIA 120347

Discovery: September 22, 2004 by Henry Roe, Michael Brown and Kristina Barkume. TNO.

Backstory: The goddess of salt water who rules the ocean and fittingly, wife of Neptune.

Possible Interpretation: Think of the adjective "salacious" and you will get an idea of what this asteroid represents: eroticism, unfiltered sexual expression and fascination, and extremes in sexual behavior.

Examples: In the natal chart of serial murderer Edmund Kemper, who murdered young college students, his mother, and his mother's best friend, and also performed heinous acts on their bodies, Salacia at 27 Sagittarius is exactly conjunct his Sun.

In the natal chart of film director Steven Spielberg, his 26 Sagittarius Sun conjoins Salacia at 25.

In the natal chart of Hollywood producer and convicted rapist Harvey Weinstein, Venus at 4 Pisces makes multiple contacts in exact opposition to Dziewanna, Psyche, and Diana, and sextiles Dick at 4 Capricorn, which exactly conjoins Salacia.

SALOME 562

Discovery: April 3, 1905 by Max Wolf.

Backstory: The seductive, sensual daughter of Herodias in the New Testament. She was known as a temptress who had to satisfy her needs. When she was spurned by John the Baptist she called for his head, which was brought to her on a platter.

Possible Interpretation: Seductive tendencies; raw sensuality; using one's own sensuality to gain favor.

Example: In the natal chart of Monica Lewinsky, who had a very public affair with President Bill Clinton in the White House, has her 9 Taurus Moon inconjunct Salome at 9 Libra.

SAPIENTIA 275

Discovery: April 15, 1888 by Johann Palisa.

Backstory: Latin word for wisdom.

Possible Interpretation: Where and how one benefits from experience, understands life's lessons and achieves wisdom, or has difficulty doing so if the asteroid is afflicted.

ASTEROIDS OUR COSMIC INFLUENCERS

Example: In the natal chart of Princess Beatrice of York, Venus at 1 Cancer partile conjoins Sapientia.

In the natal chart of activist/attorney Robert F. Kennedy, Jr., Venus at 24 Capricorn partile conjoins Sapientia.

SAPPHO 80

Discovery: May 2, 1864 by Norman R. Pogson.

Backstory: Sappho was a writer and poetess with a very romantic nature. She represents fine arts, love, and appreciation of feminine beauty.

Possible Interpretation: Represents knowledge and love of art, music, philosophy, poetry, feminism and possibly an association with feminism or lesbianism. Sadly, tormented by unrequited love, Sappho took her life by jumping off a cliff, so there may be indications of difficulty with unrequited love.

Examples: In the natal chart of rock star Courtney Love, Mars at 15 Gemini squares Sappho at 14 Virgo.

This asteroid is prominent in the natal chart of the author of this book, who is a gay writer; Sappho at 20 Libra conjoins my Mercury-Venus conjunction at 20 and 21, respectively.

Actress Elizabeth Taylor had 13 Sagittarius rising in direct opposition to Sappho.

SAUER 9248

Discovery: September 24, 1960 by C. J. van Houten and Ingrid van Houten.

Backstory: This asteroid was named for Carl G. Sauer, Jr., a flight mechanics engineer working out of the Jet Propulsion Laboratory in California that was made famous by ritual magician/occultist and engineer Jack Parsons [See CIRCE 34]. He helped develop advanced spacecraft propulsion systems.

Possible Interpretation: I don't find much info on this but I venture a guess that the asteroid may indicate special affinity or talent for engineering or aeronautics, possibly related to flight and space exploration, jet propulsion, and rocketry. The alternative meaning could relate to something being or going "sour."

Examples: British serial killer/rapist Fred West had Mercury at 1 Scorpio partile opposite Sauer. He was a common laborer, without extensive education or background in anything related to aeronautics, so the alternate "sour" may apply here to his disturbed thought processes (Mercury in the Aries degree of Scorpio). He had suffered numerous brain injuries and exhibited violent psychopathic and psychosexual behavior.

Former President George H.W. Bush had Mercury at 29 Taurus in square to Sauer at 28 Leo.

SCYLLA 155

Discovery: November 8, 1875 by Johann Palisa.

Backstory: A legendary Greek monster often paired with Charybdis. She was a beautiful sea nymph until sorceress Circe turned her into a frightening beast with six heads and snarling fangs. Two weeks after its discovery the asteroid disappeared from view and was not seen again until 1970.

ASTEROIDS OUR COSMIC INFLUENCERS

Possible Interpretation: As in the case of Charybdis, Scylla in a horoscope may indicate some physical deformity or abnormality, or a disturbing or frightening countenance.

SEDNA 90377

Discovery: November 14, 2003 by Michael Brown, Chad Trujillo and David Rabinowitz. TNO/SDO.

Backstory: Sedna is an Inuit goddess who was consigned to the depths of the ocean.

Possible Interpretation: May reference sacrifice, abandonment; being driven out of one's comfort zone; controlled by one's dark side or the subconscious mind.

Examples: British serial killer Fred West had Mars at 20 Aries partile conjunct Sedna.

Psychic trance medium Edgar Cayce had Jupiter at 2 Capricorn in partile square to Sedna in Aries.

SEKHMET 5381

Discovery: May 14, 1991 by Carolyn Shoemaker.

Backstory: The daughter of the Sun God Ra, supposedly created from the fire in his eye, she oversees the administration of justice through retribution.

Possible Interpretation: Creative and destructive force all rolled into one; balancing the scales of wrongdoing, sometimes by destruction, in order to rebuild.

Example: In the natal chart of actress Jennifer Aniston, Jupiter at 5 Libra partile conjoins Sekhmet.

B D SALERNO

Princess Beatrice of York has Mars at 9 Aries partile opposite Sekhmet.

SELQET 136818

Discovery: June 29, 1987 by R. Tucker.

Backstory: Selqet is an Egyptian scorpion goddess of magic who protects the other gods from Apophis the Destroyer. She also protects children and pregnant women from poisonous animals.

Possible Interpretation: Awareness of divine mysteries and magic; transformative powers; also associated with assisted suicide.

Example: In the natal chart of the "doctor of death" Jack Kevorkian, who helped terminally ill patients end their lives peacefully, Jupiter at 28 Aries squares Selqet at 29 Capricorn.

SEMELE 86

Discovery: January 4, 1866 by Friedrich Tietjen.

Backstory: Greek mother of Dionysus, whom she bore from an affair with Zeus. Jealous Hera tricked pregnant Semele into asking Zeus to show himself in all his might and glory. He complied, displaying a bolt of lightning that struck and killed her but spared her unborn baby.

She was the mother of Dionysus, the Greek god of wine, intoxication, wild partying, and general debauchery – sort of the mythical Greeks' answer to sex, drugs, and rock 'n' roll.

Possible Interpretation: May show the unfortunate consequences of jealousy, trickery, or third-party entanglements in relationships; domestic violence.

SEMIRAMIS 584

Discovery: January 15, 1906 by A. Kopff.

Backstory: Semiramis is a mythical queen who reigned over the Assyrian Empire for over forty years. Her name reportedly means "highest heaven" or "thunder of heaven," and she certainly made thunder on earth for those around her.

She came to the throne after poisoning her husband, King Ninus. She was bold, fiercely protective of her reign and her children, but was killed by an illegitimate son after a fight that she engaged in in order to save him.

Christian historians say that she made the practice of incest legal, and engaged in it herself; in any case, she was admired for her courage and beauty and for the reconstruction of Babylon.

Possible Interpretation: References power, fearlessness, ruthlessness; sexual deviance; how far we will go to achieve our aims; also, intense drama with children or family relations.

Example: Singer/songwriter Lady Gaga has Saturn at 9 Sagittarius directly opposite Semiramis in Gemini.

SETH 86551

Discovery: March 4, 2000 by Nigel Brady.

Backstory: Named after Seth Brady, son of the New Zealand discoverer. The asteroid may have acquired dual meaning in view of the mythical significance of its name.

Seth, or Set, was the son of the Egyptian god Geb and his queen Nut. He is a force to be feared in the Egyptian pantheon as he killed his brother Osiris, chopping him into many pieces that he scattered throughout the land. His grieving sister Isis reconstructed Osiris, including a phallus, from which she impregnated herself with his seed, giving birth to Horus.

Seth is the representative of violence, chaos, and adversity, commanding respect through fear. He is often depicted as having the head of an animal, much like Anubis, sometimes in wholly animal form. There are iterations of Seth's story. *The Egyptian Book of the Dead* refers to him as the "lord of the northern sky".

Occultist Michael Aquino founded the Temple of Set after breaking away from Anton LaVey's Church of Satan. Cults have followed Seth for centuries.

Possible Interpretation: The asteroid may represent qualities of a powerful person who commands respect but also fear; a tendency toward violence; someone who subverts their powers in directions that may be harmful to others; a charisma that attracts followers.

Examples: In the natal chart of film director Steven Spielberg, the 20 Pisces Midheaven partile squares Seth at 20 Gemini.

Pope Francis has Venus at 7 Aquarius in direct opposition to Seth.

SILA-NUNAM 79360

Discovery: February 4, 1997 by David C. Jewitt, Chad Trujillo, Jane Luu and others. TNO.

Backstory: This is a binary Kuiper Belt object with two bodies, Sila and Nunam, named after Inuit gods - Sila is the god of the sky, weather, and vitality. Nunam is the Earth goddess who created the land and its animals.

Possible Interpretation: Where we just roll with life, where we flow with ease; being in alignment with the force of nature.

Examples: In the natal chart of comedian Robin Williams, his 28 Cancer Sun exactly sextiles Sila-Nunam in Taurus.

ASTEROIDS OUR COSMIC INFLUENCERS

French President Emmanuel Macron has his 29 Sagittarian Sun partile opposite Sila-Nunam; with his government recently receiving a vote of no confidence, he will have to work hard to go with that flow.

SIRONA 116

Discovery: September 8, 1871 by Christian Peters.

Backstory: Named after the Celtic goddess of healing.

Possible Interpretation: May indicate an affinity for the healing arts; an ability or drive to fix what is broken.

Examples: In the natal chart of pop star Taylor Swift, her 21 Sagittarius Sun exactly conjoins Sirona; some of her music deals with healing from heartbreak.

Felonious hedge fund manager Bernie Madoff, with his 4 Gemini Mars in square to Sirona at 4 Virgo, convinced dozens of wealthy investors to get even wealthier by investing in his fraudulent funds.

SISYPHUS 1866

Discovery: December 5, 1972 by Paul Wild.

Backstory: Sisyphus was punished by being forced to roll a boulder up a mountain every day, only to awaken the next morning and find himself again at the bottom of the mountain. He was finally released by Heracles.

Possible Interpretation: Finding oneself in an endless cycle of monotony; getting stuck in a loop of repetitiveness; inability to learn or profit from one's mistakes.

Examples: In the natal chart of convicted sex trafficker Ghislaine Maxwell (and cohort of Jeffrey Epstein), her 14 Leo Moon partile trines Sisyphus.

Film director Steven Spielberg has his Sun at 26 Sagittarius in direct opposition to Sisyphus.

SIVA 1170

Discovery: September 29, 1930 by Eugène Delporte.

Backstory: Known as the Giver and also the Destroyer of Life, more commonly the latter, especially when afflicted by malefics. Represents the Divine Masculine of death, rebirth, the forceful removal of evil in Hindu mythology.

Possible Interpretation: May indicate creative powers in a person, for good or for ill depending on the aspects; where we are forced to change, to let go of something to build something better.

Examples: Siva was prominent in the Ascendants of several crime charts related to a string of murders in Ohio and Texas, indicating the intentional destruction of the person.

Siva at 22 Scorpio (a malevolent degree), conjoins the midpoint of the natal Venus at 20 Scorpio and Mercury at 24 Scorpio in the natal chart of serial rapist/killer Ted Bundy.

Pop star/dancer/actress Jennifer Lopez has Sun at 1 Leo and Jupiter at 1 Libra in trine and opposition aspects to Siva at 1 Aries.

Singer/songwriter Lady Gaga has Mars at 0 Capricorn exactly conjunct Siva.

SIWA 140

ASTEROIDS OUR COSMIC INFLUENCERS

Discovery: October 13, 1874 by Johann Palisa.

Backstory: Not to be confused with Siva above, she is the Slavic goddess of love and fertility.

Possible Interpretation: She represents fertility, either literal or related to an abundance of talent or creativity in the relevant areas of the horoscope.

Examples: Celebrity Oprah Winfrey has Mercury at 19 Aquarius trine Siwa at 18 Libra.

Psychic Sylvia Browne had Siwa exactly conjoined to her Midheaven at 25 Scorpio.

SKEPTICUS 6630

Discovery: November 15, 1982 by Edward Bowell.

Backstory: The asteroid was named to commemorate the 20th anniversary of the Committee for the Scientific Investigation of Claims of the Paranormal (CSICOP).

Possible Interpretation: As it sounds – where we doubt or distrust information or tend to be narrow-minded and overly judgmental. If well placed shows discernment and a keen ability to ferret out falsehoods.

Example: Russell Brand, British podcaster and media celebrity, has his Mercury at 22 Gemini trine Skepticus at 23 Aquarius.

SKULD 1130

Discovery: September 2, 1929 by Karl Wilhelm Reinmuth.

Backstory: Similar to the Three Fates in Greek mythology, Skuld was one of three fictional maidens, the Norns, living near Yggdrasill who governed the fate of humans. Skuld appears in at least two poems as a Valkyrie.

Possible Interpretation: As Skuld relates to debt, the asteroid relates to debt, either material or karmic; any debts that we are compelled to repay in order to balance out our karmic ledger.

SPARTACUS 2579

Discovery: August 14, 1977 by Nikolai Chernykh.

Backstory: Spartacus was a Thracian gladiator who escaped slavery and became a rebel leader in a slave uprising against the Romans.

Possible Interpretation: References a strong physical presence and leadership, one who may defy the status quo, a fighter for rights and equality; someone who doesn't put up with nonsense.

Example: In the natal chart of famous female aviator Amelia Earhart, her Midheaven at 19 Capricorn trines Spartacus at 18 Virgo; as a female aviator she was not afraid to challenge the male-dominated field of aviation.

SPHINX 896

Discovery: August 1, 1918 by Max Wolf.

Backstory: Secrets, riddles, and mysteries, like the aura of the Egyptian Sphinx.

Possible Interpretation: Someone who is inscrutable, keeps secrets, hides things from others; someone who is often misunderstood for these reasons.

ASTEROIDS OUR COSMIC INFLUENCERS

Examples: Jeffrey Epstein had Sphinx at 1 Aquarius conjunct his 0 Aquarius Sun, which was also conjunct the destructive Apophis at 0 and lustful Eros at 1 Aquarius.

Theoretical physicist Albert Einstein had Sphinx at 23 Cancer partile trine his Sun at 23 Pisces. He had the inside track on identifying and understanding the workings of energy in the physical world and beyond.

In the natal chart of kidnapped murder victim Charles Lindbergh, Jr., Jupiter at 29 Gemini partile opposed Sphinx. Many important aspects of that case have never been revealed, and many researchers believe that the wrong man was punished for the crime.

In the natal chart of actress Marilyn Monroe, her Saturn at 21 Scorpio exactly opposed Sphinx; her death has been shrouded in mystery, with many, myself included, believing that she was murdered.

SPLIT 12512

Discovery: April 21, 1998 by Korado Korlevič and Marino Dusič.

Backstory: Not found.

Possible Interpretation: May show where we feel divided or separated from people, places, or things; a break-up from a person, job, or situation.

STORM 12182

Discovery: October 27, 1973 by Freimut Börngen.

Backstory: Named after the 19th Century poet and novelist Theodor Storm, who is very well known in Germany.

B D SALERNO

Possible Interpretation: Again, a dual interpretation; may reference the name, writing, or German literature, or where issues tend to build up, escalate, and become chaotic.

SWINDLE 8690

Discovery: September 24, 1992 by the Spacewatch Group.

Backstory: Named after Timothy D. Swindle, a specialist in meteors.

Possible Interpretation: As a secondary meaning, it is just as it sounds – a con man, a grafter, a cheat, or a clever negotiator, someone who wheels and deals, not always by the rules.

Examples: Charles Taze Russell, founder of the Jehovah's Witness religious sect in 1870, had his 27 Aquarius Sun conjunct Swindle at 28. His religion taught that great rewards would come only to the believers of the sect after a massive migration to a new utopian reality.

In the natal chart of Branch Davidian founder David Koresh, Swindle at 7 Taurus forms a square to Mercury at 7 Leo, while Pecker at 7 Scorpio fits into a t-square; he slept with his female followers, regardless of their marital status, including teenagers.

Casey Anthony, who was acquitted of the murder of her baby daughter Caylee Marie, has Swindle at 18 Gemini in square to her 19 Pisces Ascendant; she was caught in numerous lies about the crime.

In the natal chart of Marshall Applewhite, founder of the suicidal religious group Heaven's Gate, Venus at 25 Aries trines Swindle at 24 Leo, which also forms a square to his 25 Taurus Sun which is also conjunct the malefic fixed star Caput Algol! In 1997 his 39 followers all drank poison so that their souls could be reunited in space travel with the Hale-Bopp comet.

ASTEROIDS OUR COSMIC INFLUENCERS

Allen Dulles, longest serving CIA director, (1953-1961) and a bitter enemy of President John F. Kennedy, had Moon at 4 Leo in partile square to Swindle in Taurus, which also trined his 3 Pisces Ascendant.

SWINGS 1637

Discovery: August 28, 1936 by Joseph Hunaerts.

Backstory: Named after noted Belgian astronomer Pol Swings.

Possible Interpretation: In view of the obvious reference to sexual swinging or swingers, it may indicate that tendency; may indicate something that swings or hangs; may also indicate an astronomer or someone with connections to Belgium.

SYLVIA 87

Discovery: May 16, 1866 by Norman R. Pogson.

Backstory: Roman mother of twins Romulus and Remus, also the name of the astronomer's wife. The name means "forest" in Latin. This could be one of those asteroids with dual meanings outside of the name of the person for whom it was coined, as we have already seen in previous examples.

Possible Interpretation: References motherhood, possibly of notable persons, or women by the name Sylvia; someone who enjoys nature, forestry, hiking, the outdoors.

TANTALUS 2102

Discovery: December 27, 1975 by Charles Kowal.

Backstory: Tantalus the king was condemned to hunger and thirst in punishment for tricking dinner guests into cannibalism. He made the mistake of stealing ambrosia nectar from Mount Olympus and bringing it to humans, which greatly displeased the gods.

He also insulted them by serving them parts of his dead son's body. The gods punished him by "tantalizing" him with food and drink that was just beyond his reach; he could see it and almost taste it, but was never allowed to have it.

Possible Interpretation: Where we experience frustration at not having what we want; being teased.

'Tantalus' is closely related to the word 'tantalize' and relates to things being just out of reach, never getting what you want, or teasing/tempting others, temptation without satisfaction.

Examples: Tantalus was prominent in the crime charts of several attractive gay men who were sadly lured to their deaths by sexual predators who met them at bars or parties, then seduced them and murdered them.

Ted Bundy, prolific serial killer and rapist of over 33 women, had Venus at 20 Scorpio conjunct Tantalus at 21 Scorpio. It has been said that his first victim resembled a girlfriend who had rejected him.

In the natal chart of serial rapist/murderer Randall Woodfield, who claimed over 50 victims, Mercury at 17 Capricorn squares Tantalus at 17 Aries. He could not "have" them so he controlled their fate by destroying them.

Serial killer Edmund Kemper has Tantalus at 17 Capricorn partile conjunct Mars; he was a gigantic, hulking figure who killed pretty young women because he could not have normal relationships with them.

ASTEROIDS OUR COSMIC INFLUENCERS

Tantalus at 11 Virgo exactly conjoins the Moon of pop star Madonna. She built her career around the image of a temptress, a sex goddess.

TARA 5863

Discovery: September 7, 1983 by Carolyn Shoemaker.

Backstory: She was the "Star Goddess of the Highest Wisdom," standing for peace, wisdom, spirituality, and time.

Possible Interpretation: Connection to the divine feminine, expanded consciousness, empathy, compassion, potential for high spiritual development.

Examples: Dwight D. Eisenhower, former President and Army general during World War II, had Venus at 5 Sagittarius partile conjoined to Tara.

Queen Beatrix of the Netherlands has Mercury at 18 Capricorn partile trine Tara in Taurus.

Famous female aviator Amelia Earhart had Sun at 2 Leo in square to Tara at 1 Taurus.

TATARIA 2668

Discovery: August 26, 1976 by Nikolai Chernykh.

Backstory: The pre-Mongolian empire of the Tartars was originally known as "Tataria" who at one time had conquered the world.

Possible Interpretation: I have found little on this asteroid but venture a guess that it relates to an ancestral connection to power and dominance; military influence or interests; making one's mark by conquering something.

Example: In the natal chart of fraudulent hedge fund manager Bernie Madoff, Moon at 2 Taurus conjoins Tataria at 3 Taurus.

TEHARONHIAWAKO 88611

Discovery: August 20, 2001 by the Deep Ecliptic Survey. TNO.

Backstory: Teharonhiawako is a god of maize in Iroquois (North Native American) mythology, a great grandson of the Great Spirit creation god. He was a farmer, knowledgeable about the seasons, when to plant and when to sow, and therefore conscious of time and the calendar.

Possible Interpretation: He is thus connected to timekeeping, time computing, timing, and recording timetables, including astrological time computations; farming and agriculture.

Examples: In the natal chart of heavyweight boxing champion Muhammad Ali, Jupiter at 12 Gemini is partile opposite Teharonhiawako in Sagittarius, which also forms a sextile with his 12 Aquarius Moon; he had excellent timing in the boxing ring and knew how to use it against his opponents.

Activist Cesar Chavez, who led many migrant farm workers' strikes against the big agribusiness companies, had Moon at 22 Pisces in partile trine to Teharonhiawako at 22 Scorpio; Teharonhiawako was also conjunct Diana.

TERPSICHORE 81

Discovery: September 30, 1864 by Ernst Tempel.

Backstory: One of the nine Muses, she was inspirational for ritual dance and chorals.

Possible Interpretation: May show an individual's preference for self-expression through dance, ritualistic movement, singing, or ballet.

Examples: Famous 20th Century dancer Martha Graham, who broke tradition in the art of modern dance with unconventional movements and routines, had Terpsichore in her first house tightly conjunct a Mars-Neptune-Pluto stellium. She had 5 Gemini rising with both Mars and Terpsichore at 13 Gemini in her first house. With Gemini ruling the hands/arms, many of her dance movements featured irregular and sometimes odd-looking arm and hand positions.

Elvis Presley's hip-swiveling gyrations on stage, which were initially caused by extreme stage fright, became an indelible part of his iconic image. In his natal chart Venus at 29 Capricorn sextiles Terpsichore at 29 Scorpio.

TEUTONIA 1044

Discovery: May 10, 1924 by Karl Reinmuth.

Backstory: Named after the land inhabited by the German people.

Possible Interpretation: References some connection with Germany, be it travel, culture, language, art, history, or other aspect.

TEZCATLIPOCA 1980

Discovery: June 19, 1950 by Albert Wilson and Åke Wallenquist.

Backstory: Named after an Aztec deity, it is associated with smoke and mirrors, sorcery, that which is unseen, mystery, the shadow side of things. Tezcatlipoca was also known for scrying with an obsidian mirror and prophesying the future.

B D SALERNO

Possible Interpretation: May reference someone who shrouds who they really are; fraud, trickery, deception; a mysterious aura; an attraction to the supernatural.

Examples: In the natal chart of long-time FBI director J. Edgar Hoover, his 9 Pisces Moon conjoins Tezcatlipoca at 10 Pisces. Behind the guise of law enforcement he was known to abuse his powers to exploit and manipulate countless citizens.

Dr. Anthony Fauci, former Director of the National Institute of Allergy and Infectious Diseases (NIAID), has his 13 Scorpio Moon conjunct Tezcatlipoca at 14.

THALIA 23

Discovery: December 15, 1852 by John Russell Hind.

Backstory: The Muse of Comedy, prominent in the charts of comedians and humorists.

Possible Interpretation: Where we find humor in response to circumstances; where we take a lighter approach to life; optimistic attitude.

Examples: Thalia is strongly featured in the nativity of comedienne Lucille Ball – Thalia at 25 Pisces opposes her Venus at 24 Virgo and exactly conjoins her third house cusp of communication.

Ukrainian President Volodymyr Zelenskyy has his 17 Leo Moon trine Thalia at 18 Sagittarius; prior to joining politics he was an actor and performed as a clown, which prepared him well for his next gig. Moon, Thalia, and Lust at 18 Aries form a grand trine.

In the natal chart of comedian Robin Williams, Jupiter at 13 Aries trines Thalia at 14 Leo.

ASTEROIDS OUR COSMIC INFLUENCERS

THEMIS 24

Discovery: April 5, 1853 by Annibale de Gasparis.

Backstory: A Titan goddess of natural law and divine order, daughter of Uranus and Gaea.

Possible Interpretation: May represent interest in matters of law and law enforcement, legislation and administration of civic duties.

Examples: In the natal chart of famous defense attorney Clarence Darrow, the Moon at 17 Aquarius squared Themis at 17 Taurus.

In the natal chart of infamous criminal Charles Manson, Mars at 14 Virgo, which is exactly conjunct Neptune, trines Themis at 14 Taurus. He was a defendant in one of the most sensational trials of the 20th Century.

THEREUS 32532

Discovery: August 9, 2001 by NEAT. Centaur.

Backstory: The name comes from the Greek word 'thēreios bia', meaning "beastly strength", referring to the centaurs, who were half man, half beast.

Possible Interpretation: Shows where we are in touch with our animal nature, or are gifted with physical power, strength, and boldness in body or mind.

Examples: In the natal chart of Princess Diana, Mars at 1 Virgo opposes Thereus at 2 Pisces.

Actor Matthew Perry had Mars at 12 Sagittarius partile trine Thereus at 12 Aries.

In the natal chart of psychic Sylvia Browne, her 26 Libra Sun directly opposes Thereus.

THETIS 17

Discovery: April 17, 1852 by Robert Luther.

Backstory: A Greek Nereid, mother of Achilles. A prophecy had been made that she would bear a son who would become more powerful than his father, so no god dared marry her. Instead, Peleus, a mortal, married her, much to her dismay. She bore him several children, but was dismayed that they were part mortal, so she dangled each one of them above a fire that was intended to burn out their mortal side.

Instead, the flames claimed their lives, except for that of Achilles, who was strengthened by the fire and went on to become a great warrior and Greek hero. Since Thetis had dangled him by his ankle, he was vulnerable only in that part of his body, which eventually led to his demise.

Possible Interpretation: Thetis was vain, and while her disdain for mortals was normal for a goddess, the asteroid may indicate where we think we are better than others; where we strive to maintain our status; difficulty bonding with others.

Examples: In the natal chart of pop star Lady Gaga, Venus at 24 Aries is exactly conjunct Thetis.

In the natal chart of Los Angeles celebrity defense attorney Mark Geragos, Venus at 24 Scorpio conjoins Thetis at 23.

THISBE 88

Discovery: June 15, 1866 by Christian Peters.

ASTEROIDS OUR COSMIC INFLUENCERS

Backstory: A lover of Pyramus, both of whom were characters in the Shakespearean play "A Midsummer Night's Dream". She remained at his side while he lay dying, and, reminiscent of "Romeo and Juliet," took her own life.

Possible Interpretation: May reference theatre arts, acting, drama in general; melodrama over lost love or, if afflicted, heavily grieving a lost love.

THOON 39746

Discovery: August 22, 2001 by LINEAR (Lincoln Near-Earth Asteroid Research).

Backstory: Thoon was a Lycian ally of the Trojans who followed their leader, Sarpedon, to battle in the Trojan War. He was slain by the Greek hero Odysseus.

Possible Interpretation: Bravery, loyalty to a cause.

THULE 279

Discovery: October 25, 1888 by Johann Palisa.

Backstory: Thule was a Mythical Norse land. The Thule Society, founded in August 1919, was a German occultist and Völkisch group that gave momentum to the establishment of the Nationalist Socialist Party at the end of World War I.

Possible Interpretation: May indicate a connection with Norse mythology or history, ancient pagan traditions and customs, or certain social and political beliefs, such as fascism.

Examples: Adolf Eichmann, one of Hitler's top Nazi henchmen, had Venus at 6 Aries partile conjunct Thule.

B D SALERNO

Volodymyr Zelenskyy, President of Ukraine, has Mercury at 14 Capricorn trine Thule at 15 Taurus.

THÜRINGIA 934

Discovery: August 15, 1920 by Walter Baade.

Backstory: The asteroid was named after the German state of Thüringia.

Possible Interpretation: May reference an interest in, travel to, studies or association with Germany, its culture or its language.

TISIPHONE 466

Discovery: January 17, 1901 by Max Wolf and Luigi Carnera.

Backstory: The nastiest of the Three Furies, intent on vengeance, retaliation and reprisal, nicknamed "the avenger of blood," usually dealing with vengeance over family matters.

Possible Interpretation: May indicate an attitude of vengeance toward someone when wronged, or retribution by other parties directed toward the person; possible involvement with gangs or criminal groups.

Examples: Prominent in crime charts related to the Smiley Face killings in Ohio and Texas.

In the natal chart of President-elect Trump, the Moon at 21 Sagittarius conjoins Tisiphone at 22.

TORE 97186

Discovery: November 28, 1999 by Stefano Sposetti.

ASTEROIDS OUR COSMIC INFLUENCERS

Backstory: Named after Salvatore Silanues, nicknamed "Tore," a friend of the discoverer. Although pronounced "TO-ray," in Italian, I believe the asteroid is also associated with something torn, a part of something.

Possible Interpretation: May reference an friend of Italian heritage; a part of something, a piece broken or torn off, which may be useful in crime astrology.

TORO 1685

Discovery: July 17, 1948 by Carl Wirtanen.

Backstory: A creator god of Zaire in central Africa who appeared in the form of a serpent.

Possible Interpretation: The idea of the serpent conveys aggression, strength, and power, even healing powers. It show a tendency toward violence if afflicted in the chart, or intensely passionate relationships.

Examples: In the natal chart of kidnap victim Johnny Gosch, his 24 Capricorn Moon partile squares Toro at 24 Libra.

In the natal chart of notorious drug trafficker Pablo Escobar, who was known to have psychotic episodes, Mercury at 14 Sagittarius conjoins Toro at 15 as well as Mentall. See MENTALL 7116.

The 2 Sagittarius Midheaven of Julian Assange exactly joins Toro in Leo.

In the natal chart of civil rights activist Jesse Jackson, the Midheaven at 15 Scorpio is exactly conjunct Toro.

Prince Andrew of Britain has a Venus-Mars conjunction at 28 and 27 Capricorn, respectively, conjunct Ceres at 28, which also forms a trine to Toro at 27 Taurus.

B D SALERNO

TYCHE 258

Discovery: May 4, 1886 by Robert Luther.

Backstory: Tyche was the Greek Goddess of Fortune, who became Fortuna in Roman mythology. She was often depicted with a wheel, which calls to mind the Tarot Major Arcana X Wheel of Fortune, which offers the possibility of luck, fateful changes, and opportunities coming one's way.

Possible Interpretation: It is as it sounds – where we are fortunate, feel blessed, and just seem to have good things come our way. When afflicted can show poor fortune or bad luck.

Examples: Singer/songwriter Lady Gaga has Jupiter at 8 Pisces in partile trine to Tyche in Cancer; her musical talents have earned her a fortune.

Junk bond investor and guru Michael Milken, whose scandal rocked Wall Street during the 1980s, has his Mercury at 8 Leo partile opposite Tyche in Aquarius, which forms a t-square with his 8 Taurus Midheaven.

In the natal chart of David Rockefeller, of the Rockefeller dynasty, Mercury at 26 Taurus (conjunct Algol!) squares Fortuna at 25 Leo, which conjoins Hekate at 25 Leo.

In the natal chart of mega-billionaire Warren Buffett, Mars at 1 Cancer partile conjoins Tyche.

TYPHON 42355

Discovery: February 5, 2002, by the NEAT program. Centaur.

Backstory: Typhon is one of the horrid monsters of Greek mythology: A fire-breathing, monstrous dragon with one hundred heads that hissed like snakes and venom that dripped from his eyes. He engaged in a ferocious battle with Zeus, in which he tore up Mount Aetna and threw it at him. Zeus, however, cast a thunderbolt at Typhon that pinned him underneath the mountain, killing him.

Possible Interpretation: References a powerful but ruthless person, someone whose presence may be fearsome or unsettling; a violent countenance, someone not to be crossed.

Examples: One of Hitler's highest ranking officers, Adolf Eichmann, had Saturn at 8 Pisces directly opposite Typhon. He was one of the innovators of the mass extermination of Jews during World War II.

In the natal chart of kidnap victim Johnny Gosch, Jupiter at 29 Libra partile opposes Typhon.

ULYSSES 5254

Discovery: November 7, 1986 by Eric Elst.

Backstory: Ulysses was the Roman name of the famed Greek traveler and warrior hero Odysseus, king of Ithaca, immortalized in the epic poems of Homer, the *Iliad* and the *Odyssey*. It is thought that at some point they were two separate and distinct men, who became combined over time into one multi-faceted heroic personality.

Possible Interpretation: May represent an adventurer, an explorer, a spirited person who motivates or inspires, an adventurous role model.

Examples: Astronaut John Glenn had Ulysses at 15 Scorpio sextile his Jupiter at 15 Virgo.

Astronaut Neil Armstrong had Ulysses at 8 Virgo sextile his Jupiter at 8 Cancer.

B D SALERNO

In the natal chart of Admiral Richard Byrd, explorer of the continents of Antarctica and Arctica, Mercury at 15 Scorpio partile sextiles Ulysses at 15 Capricorn.

UNDINA 92

Discovery: July 7, 1867 by Christian Peters.

Backstory: Heroine of German fairy tale.

Possible Interpretation: May indicate where we tend to fantasize, or indulge in escapism or denial; how we use imagination and creativity.

Examples: Famous producer of animated movies and founder of the Disney empire, Walt Disney, had Moon at 9 Libra in trine to Undina at 10 Aquarius.

In the natal chart of Monica Lewinsky, who had a very public affair with President Bill Clinton in the White House, has her 28 Leo Venus conjoined to Undina at 27.

URANIA 30

Discovery: July 22, 1854 by John Russell Hind.

Backstory: One of nine Muses born of Zeus and Mnemosyne, she is the Greek muse of astronomy; name means "heavenly" in Greek.

Possible Interpretation: References innovative, creative thought, spiritual/platonic love depending on its aspects; may also represent an astronomer, astrologer, or one who thinks or acts outside the box.

Examples: Astronomer/physicist Carl Sagan, who starred in the well-known educational PBS series "Cosmos," had his natal Sun at 16 Scorpio conjunct Urania.

ASTEROIDS OUR COSMIC INFLUENCERS

Urania is strongly featured in the birth chart of 20th Century psychic medium Edgar Cayce (1877-1945), who often referenced astrology in his psychic readings and would discuss the planetary influences in his clients' lives. Jupiter at 2 Capricorn partile trines Urania in Taurus.

Theoretical physicist Stephen Hawking had Urania at 12 Aquarius in partile trine to his 12 Gemini Jupiter and opposite his 13 Leo Chiron.

In the natal chart of civil rights activist Reverend Martin Luther King, Jr., his 13 Taurus Ascendant is exactly trine Urania in Virgo.

Professional motorcyclist and stunt performer Evil Knievel had Venus at 2 Sagittarius partile trine Urania in Aries; he performed uniquely original but life-threatening stunts over a period of many years, sometimes incurring severe injuries.

URDA 167

Discovery: August 28, 1876 by Christian Peters.

Backstory: A Norse figure, one of the three Nornir and the most respected. She was revered by sailors who invoked her name to keep their ships on course and helped them navigate the seas.

Possible Interpretation: She represents wisdom, stability, and understanding; assistance and guidance during challenging times.

VARDA 174567

Discovery: June 21, 2003 by Jeffrey A. Larsen. TNO.

Backstory: Varda is Queen of the Stars and of light in the J.R.R. Tolkien trilogy *Lord of the Rings*. She is bright, beautiful, and responsible for the arrangement of the stars.

B D SALERNO

Possible Interpretation: May signify a person so mentally endowed, possibly involved in astronomy, astrology, or matters pertaining to metaphysics and philosophy. Indicates a hopeful and philosophical attitude in the face of darkness and chaos.

Examples: Eleanor Roosevelt, wife of President Franklin D. Roosevelt, had her 16 Sagittarius Ascendant in trine to Varda at 16 Leo. During the Great Depression and World War II she devoted herself to improving the morale of the country during difficult times.

Writer Stephen King's Ascendant at 11 Libra is partile opposite Varda.

In the natal chart of Hindu spiritual leader Yogananda, Mercury at 23 Sagittarius trines Varda at 24 Leo.

VARUNA 20000

Discovery: November 2000 by Robert McMillan. TNO.

Backstory: Named after a major Hindu deity and Vedic god, originally on the level of creator of Heaven and Earth, but later reassigned to god of the waters, mainly, rain. He rides upon a fish or sea monster, or in a chariot drawn by seven horses. In southern India his assistance is still prayed for in times of drought. His name equates to "he who covers" in Sanskrit.

Possible Interpretation: Varuna may represent a powerful person, possibly extremely wealthy and successful, also, a strong leader; one who possesses deep understanding of cosmic law; one whose vision encompasses vast knowledge.

Examples: Pop star Madonna's Mars at 15 Taurus exactly conjoins Varuna; she has extensively studied the Kabbalah and mysticism.

In the natal chart of whistleblower Julian Assange, his 2 Sagittarius Ascendant partile opposes Varuna, which also conjoins Crantor.

ASTEROIDS OUR COSMIC INFLUENCERS

In the natal chart of wrestling champion turned Governor of Minnesota turned conspiracy theorist Jesse Ventura, his 5 Virgo Venus exactly trines Varuna in Taurus.

VATICANA 416

Discovery: May 4, 1896 by Auguste Charlois.

Backstory: One of Rome's seven hills.

Possible Interpretation: The interpretation may deal with the Vatican itself, or some connection to the clergy, Italy, or a powerful religious institution.

VELLEDA 126

Discovery: November 5, 1872 by Paul Henry.

Backstory: A German princess who led in the uprising of the region of Batavia against the Roman army.

Possible Interpretation: A strong leader in warfare or politics; a maverick or rebel.

VESTA 4

Discovery: March 29, 1807 by Heinrich Wilhelm Olbers.

Backstory: Roman goddess of home, hearth, and family whose name derived from the Sanskrit word "vas," meaning "shine" or "bright". She was born of Cronus and Rhea and was the last swallowed child to be freed from Cronus' stomach by Zeus. Having experienced such childhood trauma she took an oath never to have children and to remain chaste. In spite of hot pursuit by both Zeus and Apollo, she stayed true to her promise; in those days women who violated their oaths of chastity would be slowly buried alive. The Vestal Virgins were a cult of followers of women who pledged to maintain their chastity.

As keeper of the hearth, Vesta's image was honored in public places throughout the Roman Empire.

Possible Interpretation: Vesta's symbol is the fire of the hearth; she guards over the home and the community. However, she is deeply linked to sexual mores as well, which is something to take account of in studying the asteroid's placement in the nativity.

In a chart shows where the person is a good provider or caretaker of the matter represented in the relevant house and sign. Where we guard or protect that which is important, our families, roots, communities, and so forth. But being associated with virginity also shows where the individual may foster repressed sexual feelings and identity; attitudes toward sexual behavior, and possible psychological issues concerning societal sexual norms.

Examples: Tennis champion Martina Navratilova has her Moon at 12 Aries in partile trine to Vesta in Sagittarius.

Former Mafia hitman-turned-witness Sammy "the Bull" Gravano has Mars at 20 Aquarius partile trine Vesta in Libra; he derived much of his identity from the "family" of organized crime.

Popular media psychologist Dr. Joyce Brothers had Vesta at 26 Virgo exactly trine her Taurus Ascendant.

Prince Andrew of Britain's Royal Family has 22 Sagittarius Vesta trine his 22 Aries Midheaven.

Golf champion Tiger Woods has Venus at 28 Scorpio trine Vesta at 28 Pisces.

ASTEROIDS OUR COSMIC INFLUENCERS

Supermodel Gisele Bundchen has Mercury at 15 Cancer exactly opposite Vesta.

VILLON 10140

Discovery: September 19, 1993 by Eric Elst.

Backstory: Named after François Villon, French poet of the 15th Century.

Possible Interpretation: May reference French literature, France, or a French person. An alternate application for the name might be "villain," although I have not noted interpretations along these lines. Accordingly, the reference would be a bad person, a troublemaker.

VULCANO 4464

Discovery: First discovery January 2, 1860 by Urbain LeVerrier, who thought the body was a planet; in 1966 the body was determined to be an asteroid. There is also a Uranian planet, Vulkanus, named for the same mythical figure.

Backstory: Vulcano orbits the Sun inside the orbit of Mercury, the planet closest to the Sun, and is exposed to astronomically high temperatures. It is fitting that it was named after the mythical Vulcan who was a master blacksmith, crafting all kinds of metal into weaponry and utensils, and thus references expertise with metals, mechanical engineering, working with fire or sources of extreme heat.

Vulcano is associated with the Greek Hephaistos, and was also physically deformed as the result of being hurled to earth by Jupiter for trying to save his mother from Jupiter's advances.

Possible Interpretation: The asteroid may indicate someone skilled with fire or metallurgy, mechanical engineering, heating, combustion, aerospace, or energy sources; someone whose energy and passion radiate heat. I also believe there is some connection to the transformative processes of alchemy.

Examples: In the natal chart of SpaceX and Tesla founder Elon Musk, Vulcano at 4 Cancer conjoins his 5 Cancer Sun.

WALKÜRE 877

Discovery: September 13, 1915 by Russian astronomer Grigory Neujmin.

Backstory: A female spirit in Norse mythology immortalized by the opera *Die Walküre* by German composer Richard Wagner.

Possible Interpretation: References strife among family members, notably, fathers and daughters, over their choices of love partners, and can also involve disputes between siblings.

WALPURGA 256

Discovery: April 3, 1886 by Johann Palisa.

Backstory: Saint Walpurga, much revered in pagan lore, was an Anglo-Saxon missionary to the Frankish Empire. She was canonized by Pope Adrian II in 870. Her feast day is April 30 or "Walpurgisnacht", also a high holy day revered by certain groups and cults, including the Nazis.

The spirit of Walpurga was invoked for protection by those enduring harsh storms, and by sailors during difficult travels at sea.

Possible Interpretation: There is also a deity Walpurga, responsible for the forests, grain, and natural springs, much akin to the Roman Diana. Based on this information I venture a guess that this asteroid conveys similar meaning to that of Diana – a deep connection to nature, wildlife, hiking, ecology, a naturalist or environmentalist.

YARILO 2273

Discovery: March 6, 1975 by Lyudmila I. Chernykh.

Backstory: Named after a Slavic god of spring, fertility, agriculture, and war, and the son of Perun and Mokosz.

Possible Interpretation: References vitality, personal magnetism, positivity, and an attraction to nature.

ZEUS 5731

Discovery: November 4, 1988 by Carolyn Shoemaker.

Backstory: Zeus, the most powerful Greek Olympian, whose Roman counterpart is Jupiter, renowned for his multiple love affairs and offspring with dozens of goddesses, nymphs, and mortals alike. A very powerful, influential, and prolific figure, successful, desired and loved by many, but not without human failings and questionable behavior.

Zeus is also a Uranian planetary body; it appears without a number in asteroid software.

Possible Interpretation: Zeus prominent in the nativity can indicate strong leadership drive and abilities; a desire for power, a tendency to think that the rules don't apply to them; strong sexual drive and interest in procreating; highly creative, but can also be highly destructive as the person sees fit. Zeus would have a kingly approach to things, quite possibly with the know-how to work or compete with other powerful entities.

B D SALERNO

Example: Lieutenant Colonel of U.S. Army Psychological Operations, and founder of Temple of Set Michael Aquino, had his 22 Libran Sun sextile Zeus at 22 Leo.

ZHULONG 472235

Discovery: April 4, 2014 by Pan-STARRS. TNO/SDO.

Backstory: Also called Enlightener of the Dark or Torch Dragon, he is a Chinese mythological creature with a human face and a bright red serpent's body.

Possible Interpretation: References superior power, strength and ability to influence and enlighten others, as a great teacher or role model.

Examples: In the natal chart of Princess Diana, Jupiter at 5 Aquarius is partile opposite Zhulong.

Reverend Martin Luther King, Jr., civil rights activist, had Venus at 10 Pisces in partile trine to Zhulong in Cancer.

In the natal chart of novelist Stephen King, Mars at 24 Cancer partile conjoins Zhulong.

ZOOZVE 524522

Discovery: November 11, 2002 by LONEOS [Lowell Observatory Near-Earth Observation Group].

Backstory: This odd name evolved from the original designation of the asteroid, which was 2002VE. It is a quasi-satellite of Venus, but has a very irregular path approaching the Sun, and is therefore expected to just derail from its orbit some day.

ASTEROIDS OUR COSMIC INFLUENCERS

Possible Interpretation: I venture a guess that this is something akin to Venus' misbehaving little sister, so it may indicate where someone expresses negative Venusian qualities, such as vanity, excessive partying, spending, socializing, etc.

REFERENCES

Cavendish, Richard, ed. *Mythology: An Illustrated Encyclopedia.* (New York: Barnes and Noble Books, 1992).

D'Aulaire, Ingri and Edgar Parin D'Aulaire. *D'Aulaires' Book of Greek Mythology.* (New York: Delacorte Press, 1962).

Evans, Lady Hestia. *Mythology: The Gods, Heroes, and Monsters of Ancient Greece.* (Cambridge: Candlewick Press, 1825).

George, Demetra and Douglas Bloch. *Asteroid Goddesses: The Mythology, Psychology, and Astrology of the Re-Emerging Feminine.* (Lake Worth: Nicolas-Hays, Inc., 2003).

Jordan, Michael. *Encyclopedia of Gods.* (New York: Facts On File Inc., 1993).

Keenan, Sheila. *Gods, Goddesses, and Monsters: An Encyclopedia of World Mythology.* (New York: Scholastic Inc., 2000).

Morford, Mark P.O. and Robert J. Lenardon. *Classical Mythology.* (New York: Oxford University Press, 2007).

I am very grateful to the following astrologers, bloggers, and contributors to the websites below for providing vital information on the asteroids.

www.alexasteroidastrology.com[7]

---

7. http://www.alexasteroidastrology.com

www.darkstarastrology.com[8]

www.linda-goodman.com[9]

www.markandrewholmes.com[10]

www.minorplanetcenter.org[11]

www.serennu.com[12]

www.theblissfulstar.tumblr.com[13]

---

8. http://www.darkstarastrology.com

9. http://www.linda-goodman.com

10. http://www.markandrewholmes.com

11. http://www.minorplanetcenter.org

12. http://www.serennu.com

13. http://www.theblissfulstar.tumblr.com

Also by B D SALERNO

Desperate Rites
Desperate Rites: Astrology and the Occult in the Richard Speck Murders

Standalone
Richard Speck and the Eight Nurses: Deconstructing A Mass Murder
Richard Speck and the Eight Nurses: Deconstructing A Mass Murder
Anywhere But Here: Confessions of A Pisces Moon
Asteroids Our Cosmic Influencers

About the Author

BD Salerno received her undergraduate and graduate education at Rutgers University and her secondary education in New York City, where she trained in medical massage therapy, acupuncture, and other holistic modalities. Her eclectic interests – alternative healing, metaphysics, and true crime - focus on understanding what makes things tick.

Salerno combined her love for astrology with her fascination for true crime and published two books on the astrology of crime: *Forensics by the Stars* in 2012, and *Exploring Forensic Astrology* in 2016. The astrology of the nurses' mass murder was what clued her in to the notion that all was not what it had always seemed.

In this book, three years in the making, Salerno has taken a deep dive into a crime that disturbed her greatly as a young girl – the mass murder of eight nurses by Richard Speck in 1966 Chicago. Her findings were nothing short of shocking, leading her to the conclusion that the crime did not happen as we were told. We didn't get the true story the first time around. You can read it now here.

www.ingramcontent.com/pod-product-compliance
Lightning Source LLC
Chambersburg PA
CBHW031625160426
43196CB00006B/288